Physical Characteristics of the Wire Fox Terrier

(from the American Kennel Club breed standard)

Tail: Set on rather high and carried gaily. It should be of good strength and substance and of fair length.

Back: Short and level with no appearance of slackness.

Hindquarters: Strong and muscular, quite free from droop or crouch; the thighs long and powerful, stifles well curved and turned neither in nor out; hocks well bent and near the ground should be perfectly upright and parallel.

Loins: Muscular and very slightly arched. The bitch may be slightly longer in couplings than the dog.

Coat: Broken, the hairs having a tendency to twist, and are of dense, wiry texture—like coconut matting—the hairs growing so closely and strongly together that, when parted with the fingers, the skin cannot be seen.

Size and Proportion: A full-sized, well balanced dog should not exceed 15.5 inches at the withers—the bitch being proportionately lower—nor should the length of back from withers to root of tail exceed 12 inches, while to maintain the relative proportions, the head should not exceed 7.25 inches or be less than 7 inches.

Feet: Round, compact, and not large—the pads tough and well cushioned, and the toes moderately arched and turned neither in nor out.

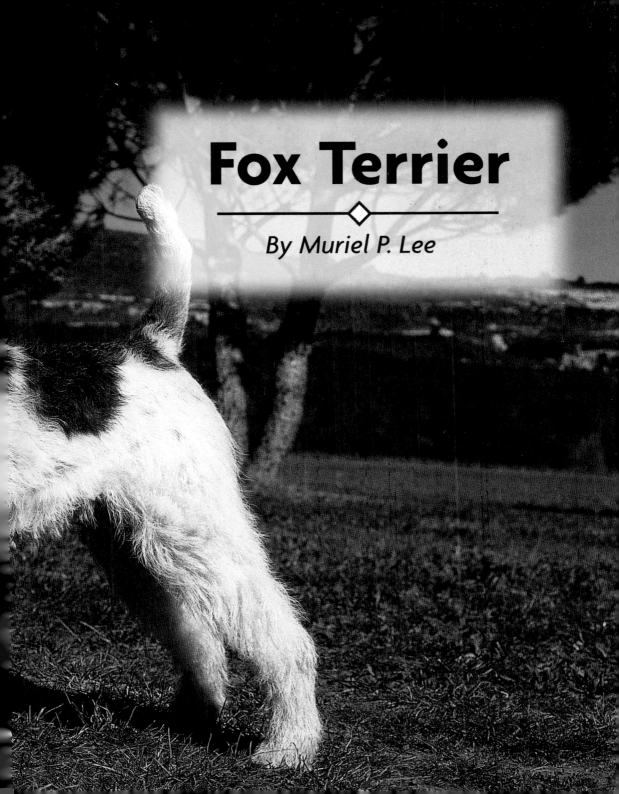

Fox Terrier

By Muriel P. Lee

Contents

Training Your Fox Terrier   92

Begin with the basics of training the puppy and adult dog. Learn the principles of house-training the Fox Terrier, including the use of crates and basic scent instincts. Enter Puppy Kindergarten and introduce the pup to his collar and leash and progress to the basic commands. Find out about obedience classes and other activities.

Healthcare of Your Fox Terrier   117

By Lowell Ackerman DVM, DACVD
Become your dog's healthcare advocate and a well-educated canine keeper. Select a skilled and able veterinarian. Discuss pet insurance, vaccinations and infectious diseases, the neuter/spay decision and a sensible, effective plan for parasite control, including fleas, ticks and worms.

Showing Your Fox Terrier   148

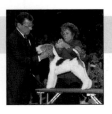

Step into the center ring and find out about the world of showing pure-bred dogs. Here's how to get started in AKC shows, how they are organized and what's required for your dog to become a champion. Take a leap into the realms of obedience trials, agility, earthdog events and tracking tests.

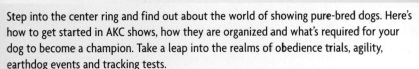

KENNEL CLUB BOOKS: **FOX TERRIER**
ISBN: 1-59378-272-1

Copyright © 2005 • Kennel Club Books, LLC
308 Main Street, Allenhurst, NJ 07711 • USA
Cover Design Patented: US 6,435,559 B2 • Printed in South Korea

Photography by Isabelle Français
with additional photographs by

Mary Bloom, Paulette Braun, T.J. Calhoun, Alan and Sandy Carey, Carolina Biological Supply, Isabelle Français, Carol Ann Johnson, Bill Jonas, Dr. Dennis Kunkel, Tam C. Nguyen, Phototake, Jean Claude Revy and Karen Taylor.

Illustrations by Reneé Low and Patricia Peters.

The publisher wishes to thank Rick Chashoudian, Sam Draper, Virginia Matanic, Kathleen Reges and all of the owners whose dogs are illustrated in this book.

The most handsome terrier in the world, the Fox Terrier sporting its classic wire coat is a hard dog to beat—in the show ring, in a loving home and on the field. The Wire Fox Terrier is a true "forever" dog.

HISTORY OF THE

FOX TERRIER

The Fox Terrier, whether he is in his smooth coat or all dressed up in his wire jacket, is among the most handsome of all the terriers. Mischievous, active, game and entertaining...all words that describe this wonderful English dog. At one time he was a working dog, running with the horses and hounds, chasing down vermin and bolting foxes. His instincts are not lost to him now, but he is content to have his family as his companions and a comfy sofa for his bed. This may not be the dog for everyone, because of his very active ways, but if you like a busy and plucky dog, one who fits easily into city or country life, this may just be the dog for you.

An old adage says, "Dogs may come and dogs may go, but the Fox Terrier goes on forever." Indeed, once you give your heart to a Fox Terrier, it will remain true and steadfast to the breed for a lifetime.

ORIGIN OF THE FOX TERRIER

The Fox Terriers originated in the hunting kennels of England, and their origins trace back a long way through history. Although the early history is murky, modern Fox

Int. Ch. Gallant Fox of Wildoaks was one of the outstanding dogs of his time. He was born in 1929 and was owned by Mrs. R. C. Bondy of New York.

A beautiful painting from *The Illustrated Book of the Dog*, published in 1881. It shows the characteristics of the breed at that time.

Eng. Ch. Dame Fortune, owned by Mr. F. Redmond, in a painting by Arthur Wardle, *circa* 1901.

Terrier history is fairly straightforward, dating back to the 1860s.

The Fox Terrier belongs to the group of dogs described as terriers, from the Latin word *terra*, meaning earth. The terrier is a dog that has been bred to work beneath the ground to drive out small and large vermin, rodents and other animals that can be a nuisance to country living.

All of the dogs in the Terrier Group originated in the British Isles with the exception of the Cesky Terrier, which, of course, originated in Czechoslovakia. Many of the

terrier breeds were derived from a similar ancestor; as recently as the mid-1800s, the terriers fell roughly into two basic categories: the rough-coated, short-legged dogs which tended to come from Scotland; and the longer-legged, smooth-coated dogs which were bred in England and Wales. The terriers, although they may differ in type, all have the same character, being game dogs

that go after vermin. They also make good companions for their masters.

As early as 1735, the *Sportsman's Dictionary* described the terrier as "a kind of hound, used only or chiefly for hunting the fox or badger. He creeps into the ground and then nips and bites the fox and badger, either by tearing them in pieces with his teeth, or else hauling them and pulling them by force out of their lurking holes." The terrier background is obscure but what was certain in the 1700s and early 1800s was that there was no definite breed of "terrier," but that the dogs were bred to go to ground with courage and convic-

The Totteridge Eleven as painted by Arthur Wardle in 1898. These dogs are all excellent examples of the breed in those days.

tion. Those who were unable to do the job were destroyed, and those who could do the proper work were bred to one another with little regard for type. "Unless they were fit and game for the purpose, their heads were not kept long out of the huge butt of water in the stable yard." Those who bred and kept dogs had a specific purpose of work for their particular breed—long legs for speed, short legs for going to ground; double-coated for protection against the elements, and all terriers have a powerful set of teeth.

In 1862 the first class for Fox Terriers was offered at the Islington Agricultural Hall show, and there were over 20 entered. The winner was described as "without pedigree,

coarse looking but workmanlike and black and tan in colour." Later in the year a class was offered at the Birmingham show as "white and other smooth-haired English Terriers except black and tan."

By the following year three dogs were entered, and although of

Eden Exquisite, produced by the Crackley Kennels, a supreme producer of fine Fox Terriers, was sent to America. Shown in this photo at seven and a half months of age, she was referred to as one of the best bitch puppies ever seen.

> ### FOX TERRIER VICTORIES
> Crufts Dog Show, established in 1891, reigns as Britain's premier canine spectacular and attracts the best dogs in the UK. The Wire Fox Terrier has claimed the honor of Supreme Champion of Crufts on three occasions: in 1962, Eng. Ch. Crackwyn Cockspur, owned by H. L. Gill; in 1975, Eng. Ch. Brookewire Brandy of Layven, owned by Messrs Benelli and Dondini; and in 1978 Eng. Ch. Harrowhill Huntsman, owned by Miss E. Howles.

a decade, had become the most popular breed in England. By 1890, Rawdon Lee, who wrote the most respected history on the Fox Terrier up to that time, was able to make up a list of the ten finest Fox Terriers in England, all sound, stylish dogs that were consistent in type.

The Smooth Fox Terrier was probably derived from the smooth-coated Black and Tan Terrier from Wales, Derbyshire and Durham, with crosses to the Bull Terrier, the Greyhound and the Beagle (for color), along with the old English White Terrier. The smooth-coated dogs had more Bull Terrier than did the Wire Fox Terrier. The Wires were probably descended from the rough-coated Black and Tan Terrier and later crossed with the Smooth Fox, with the Smooth adding refinement to the Wire as well as bringing down its size. The wirehaired dogs were more prevalent in the North of England and South Wales, while the Smooths were found throughout England. Early on when the

doubtful pedigrees, these were the three dogs to which the modern Fox Terrier can trace back his heritage. The dogs were Old Jock, Tartan and Trap. Jock, an 18-pound, almost all-white dog, was owned by Mr. Wooton and was shown over a 9-year span until the age of 11 years. Tartan, bred by Mr. Stevenson, had no pedigree but produced a nice line of notable Smooths. He was so muscular that he was called the "Pocket Hercules." Trap's lineage probably traced back to the Oakley Hunt strain, the old black and tan English Terriers with strong markings, bred by the Master of the Oakley Hunt. Classes for the Wire Fox Terrier were not held until 1873 at the Crystal Palace show.

The breed was well received, and in 1872 there were 276 Fox Terriers entered at the Nottingham show, which included 109 bitches! The Fox Terrier, in a matter of only

Ch. Crackley Surethin, born in 1932, was one of the most expensive sires of the time.

bristly coat that can have a light wave (not curly) with a soft undercoat, thick enough so that skin cannot be seen through the coat. This is a coat that requires considerable grooming. The Smooth, with its short, straight jacket, has nowhere to hide any faults as his thick, rather coarse short coat reveals every crevice of every muscle and tendon.

An early pillar of the breed was Belgrave Joe, whelped in 1868, from the Leicester Kennels. Joe was considered to be the most perfect Fox Terrier produced up to that time. He lived to be 19 years of age and produced many champions. Rawdon Lee wrote about Belgrave Joe in 1890, "He handed his good

The dapper Mr. Francis Redmond with his Smooth-coated Fox Terrier named Daddy. This photo was originally published in 1902.

Smooths and Wires were interbred, you could get both types of coats in the same litter.

The Wire differs from the Smooth in coat only. The Wire has a

CANIS LUPUS

"Grandma, what big teeth you have!" The gray wolf, a familiar figure in fairy tales and legends, has had its reputation tarnished and its population pummeled over the centuries. Yet it is the descendants of this much-feared creature to which we open our homes and hearts. Our beloved dog, *Canis domesticus*, derives directly from the gray wolf, a highly social canine that lives in elaborately structured packs. In the wild, the gray wolf can range from 60 to 175 pounds, standing between 25 and 40 inches in height.

looks down to his sons and grandsons and great-grandsons and granddaughters. At the present time there are few leading Fox Terriers that have not, on one side or another, some drop or more of the old dog's blood coursing through their veins." Joe's skeleton resides in the members' room of The Kennel Club in London.

In 1876 the Fox Terrier Club in England was formed and a standard for the breed was written. The Smooths and the Wires each had separate stud book registers. In the early years breeding between the two varieties was common, primarily in order to give the Wire the clean lines and the refined head of the Smooth. Correct type in both varieties was well established many years ago, and crossbreeding between the two varieties has not been done for decades.

The breed became more stabilized, as now all proper breeders had a written picture of what the breed should look like. By following the standard, more unifor-

mity was brought to the breed as breeders realized that all pups in a litter should look alike as well as being of the same type as their sire and dam.

Her Grace Kathleen, Duchess of Newcastle, was the first president of the Fox Terrier Club; there was a total of 21 members. Their first show was held in May 1877 with an entry of 220 dogs. The popularity of the breed continued to rise and by 1888 there were 52 classes for Smooth and Wires and the entry was 434 at the Sheffield show.

There have been many exceptional Fox Terrier kennels in Britain, and a few should be mentioned in this short history. The Duchess of Newcastle bred many top Wires in her Notts kennels. Of note were Eng. Ch. Cackler of Notts, who was the sire of many champions, and Eng. Ch. Conald of Notts. The Duchess was a great lover of the breed and did much to promote it in England. Francis Redmond bred Eng. Ch. Donna Fortuna in 1896, who, in five years of showing, was never defeated. This was during a time when the competition was extremely keen in Smooths. She was considered for many years to be the greatest Smooth ever bred. Upon her show retirement, she was placed with a gamekeeper and she was said to have been a game and clever worker against ferret, badger and fox.

George Raper, a breeder of Wires, was a top handler,

Eng. Ch. Talavera Jupiter belonged to the famous Captain Phipps. Many Fox Terriers of the same bloodline are found among American dogs.

Eng. Ch. Dusky Siren was born in 1903 and was painted in 1905 by Maud Earl. If the painting is accurate, the dogs of those days were quite different from modern Fox Terriers.

conditioner of Wires and a renowned judge in the late 1800s and early 1900s. His Eng. Ch. Go Bang, bred by G. W. Norman, was campaigned from 1895 to 1898 and won the Fifty Guinea Challenge Cup eight times, a feat never duplicated. When Go Bang was sold to Major Carnochan in America, Raper, always the consummate showman, personally delivered the dog to American shores where Go Bang was declared to be the best Wire seen in America up to that time.

Great Wires of the 1920s were Eng. Ch. Warrington Bridegroom, bred by Mr. F. Pearce and exported to the United States. He was the sire of eight American champions and many English champions. Bridegroom sired the great Eng. Ch. Fountain Crusader, who was called the "wonder coated" dog. Eng. Ch. Fountain Crusader was said to be a nearly faultless dog with the correct size, heavy hound markings and a great personality. He sired 23 champions, including the great Eng.

Three champion Fox Terriers owned by the Duchess of Newcastle.

Ch. Talavara Simon. Simon sired many show and stud dogs in both Great Britain and America and was considered the outstanding influence on the modern Wire Fox Terrier. Simon was handled to perfection by Bob Barlow, owned by George Raper. His double grandson, Crackley Starter, made a major

Her Grace, the Duchess of Newcastle, showing one of her dogs. The dog, Cracknels Verdict of Notts, won eight first prizes.

Bowes Brevity was the sire of over 100 winners, including two champions, and was second best stud dog at the Wire Fox Terrier Club. Unfortunately the dog was tampered with, and his show career ended prematurely. The culprit was never found.

impact on the Wires in America. Simon was also the sire of Int. Ch. Gains Great Surprise, who was considered the best show bitch up to that time. It was written that Simon dominated the Wires for generations and improved the breed to the point of revolutionizing it.

Miss Linda Beck started breeding and showing Smooths and Wires in the mid-1930s. She linebred her own stud dogs and developed the Newmaidly line. She continued showing until 1991 and died in 1992 at the age of 84. Brazilian Ch. Newmaidly For'ard won 50 all-breed Bests in Show. The American handler Wood Wornall imported Eng. Ch. Newmaidly Gladiator, who was thought to be a prime example of what a Smooth Fox Terrier should be.

Mr. Bob Barlow, known as "Mr. Fox Terrier," was considered to be the premier breeder, handler, scout and all-round authority on the Wire. He was a major influence in discovering great dogs in the 1920s and 1930s. His remarkable grooming skills changed the breed forever. He handled many of Eng. Ch. Talavara Simon's grandsons and granddaughters, including the great Eng. Ch. Crackley Starter. He exported dogs to America and imported their offspring back to Great Britain.

Dr. R. M. Miller, Boreham Kennels, bred many Smooth champions, starting with Eng. Ch. Boreham Bister in 1931. He continued an active breeding program through the 1980s. Mr. Clanachan of the Maryholm

Circa 1925, when the first Kodak film was produced which could take photos at 1,000th of a second, Mr. C. C. Walters of the RSPCA, a Terrier fancier, posed for this picture. This photo was printed in several books and magazines because Walters was so well known. It gave impetus to the popularity of the breed.

The photo to the left shows a trainer with his Fox Terrier jumping as high as the trainer is tall, into the water.

Kennels bred Wires as well as Smooths and has been described as one of the leading breeders and exhibitors of Fox Terriers in Britain. Many champions have come out of his kennel including Ch. Maryholm Spun Gold in 1947, who became a top stud dog for the kennel.

Watteau Kennels, started in the 1900s by Mr. Frank Calvert, was eventually taken over by his daughter, Mrs. Mary Blake, and granddaughter, Mrs. Antonia Thornton. This very active kennel has been the standard bearer for the Smooths for many decades. The influence that this kennel has made on Smooths in the British Isles and

LEFT: Int. Ch. Thet Timber, born in 1928, held the world's record as having earned championships in the US, England and the Continent. RIGHT: Flornell Saloon was considered to be one of the best Fox Terriers in the breed, *circa* 1930.

in America has been tremendous, not only through the dogs that have been bred but also through the daughters and sons and granddaughters and grandsons who have also been Best in Show winners on both sides of the Atlantic.

The number of remarkable Fox Terriers that have been bred in the British Isles and who have made their mark upon the breed is tremendous, and the list is far too

A top American sire imported from Finland, here's Ch. Starring Joint of Santeric, winning at a Fox Terrier specialty show. Owners, Kathy Reges and Ric Chashoudian.

extensive to include in this short history. An early history of the breed can be read in Rawdon Lee's beautiful book *The Fox Terrier*. This was published in the late 1800s, so a copy may be difficult to find.

FOX TERRIERS IN AMERICA

The first Fox Terrier to arrive in America was shown in New York in 1883. In 1885 the American Fox Terrier Club was founded and held its first show in 1886 with an impressive entry of 75 Smooths and only 4 Wires. The entry was made up of predominantly English imports. In 1892 the first English Champion was imported into America. The 1926 winner of Westminster was Ch. Signal Circuit of Halleston, owned by Stanley Halle and Halleston Kennels. At Westminster in 1929 there was an astounding Fox Terrier entry of 306 (there has never been, in any breed, another entry that large at that show) which shows the tremendous popularity the breed enjoyed in the early part of the 20th century.

Making dog history in the early 1900s, Smooth Fox Ch. Warren Remedy, owned by Winthrop Rutherford, won the prestigious Best in Show award at Westminster Kennel Club dog show for three consecutive years, 1907, 1908 and 1909, a feat that has never been repeated by any dog of any breed before or since. Mr. Rutherford was a powerful influence in the breed and served as president of the American Fox Terrier Club from 1896 to 1920 and again from 1931 until his death in 1944. His Warren kennels provided foundation stock for many other kennels of the time. F. H. Farwell, Sabine Kennels in Texas, finished nearly 40 champions, including Ch. Sabine Rarebit, Best in Show at Westminster Kennel Club in 1910.

Many of the early supporters in America were individuals of wealth who were able to import the best British dogs and, before too long, they brought along the handlers of these dogs. Among those handlers was the great Percy Roberts, who became a highly regarded all-breed judge and was considered to be one of the great dog men of the 20th century. During the 1920s and 1930s many of the top Wires and Smooths were brought to America.

In the 1930s a particularly exciting Smooth Fox reached American shores, Ch. Nornay Saddler, bred by Mr. and Mrs.

Frank Coward of England. Saddler was purchased by Jim Austin of Wissaboo Kennels. During the previous decade interest in the Wire Fox had been increasing but with the appearance of this outstanding Smooth, the tide in popularity again turned back to the Smooth. Ch. Nornay Saddler won Best in Show at the prestigious Morris and Essex show, among his 55 all-breed Bests in Shows. He was a very prepotent sire and made a tremendous impact upon the Smooth Fox Terriers.

Smooth breeders in the very late 1930s and 1940s were many. Mrs. Barbara Lowe Fallas of Anderly Kennels imported quality dogs from England in addition to breeding excellent stock. Thirty-nine champions came out of her kennel, of which 31 were

This is what the American version of the Wire-haired dog looked like in the early 1930s. Flornell Spicy Bit of Halleston, owned by Mr. Stanley Halle, was proclaimed the Best in Show at the Westminster Kennel Club show held in Madison Square Garden, New York, in February 1934. He triumphed over 3,000 contenders.

homebred. Norman, Mary and Chris Bowker, Bowmanor Kennels, got their foundation bitch from Mrs. Fallas. Bowmanor's Dolly of Beafox became a top-producing Smooth dam, a record that still stands well to this day.

The very famous Foxden Kennel of Mr. and Mrs. James Farrell, Jr. of Darien, CT, starting in the 1930s, imported the best Smooths from Great Britain, in addition to breeding outstanding stock for many decades. Ch. Higrola Horatio of Britlea sired 28 champions; Ch. Foxden Warpaint and his son Ch. Foxden Warspite were outstanding winners as well as top producers. The foundation stock of many kennels came from Foxden, as the Farrells thought it

important to let others use their dogs. Mrs. Farrell served many terms as president of the American Fox Terrier Club.

Outstanding winning Smooths were Ch. Flornell Spicy Bit of Halleston, who won Westminster in 1934, and his kennelmate Ch. Flornell Spicy Piece, who won the show in 1937. Both dogs were owned by Stanley Halle of Halleston Kennels in New York and handled by Percy Roberts.

Although World War II interrupted breeding and show activities in the US, as it had in Europe, by the late 1940s both were in high gear again. In the 1950s the exceptional Smooth Fox Ch. Ttarb the Brat of Foxhill, bred by Mr. and Mrs. D. C. Brat and owned by Dr. John

This top show dog roars to name of "Leo." This is Ch. Kathrich Santeric Windfall, winning one of many Group 1's. Owners, Kathy Reges and Ric Chashoudian.

Van Zandt and Ed Dalton, came onto the scene. Brat was handled by Ric Chashoudian. A formidable opponent in the ring, the Brat racked up many wins. Brat was a great show dog as well as a great producer.

Mrs. Winifred Stout, Quissex Kennels in Rhode Island, produced and showed many winners in the 1960s and 1970s. Ch. Foxden Hercules sired over 20 champions, and Ch. Quissex Deacon produced 32 champions including 3 Group winners. Well over 100 champions have come from this kennel, and Mrs. Stout is still very active in the breed.

The Toofox Kennels in Texas, of Bill and Betsy Dossett, started with their foundation bitch Ch. Miss Me Too Spot, who was the top Smooth bitch in 1976 and the top-producing bitch in 1979. Ch. Toofox Lady Evelyn produced 15 champions. The Toofox dogs have done exceptionally well in the show ring as well as in the whelping box. Joe and Murrel Purkhiser of Caribe Kennels in Texas purchased Ch. Toofox the Caribe Chief Spy from the Dossetts; he completed his championship by eight months of age and won four all-breed Bests in Show, in addition to the Breed at the famous Montgomery County Kennel Club show in 1985.

Virginia Matanic of the Briarlea Kennels handles all her own homebred dogs. She has finished dozens of her own Wires in the show ring.

Dedicated breeders of the Smooth Fox Terrier are carrying on with the traditions of their predecessors and producing top-notch Smooths. Joseph Vaudo and Elizabeth Tobin, Bluestone Kennels from Massachusetts, are doing well with their dogs in this new century. Ch. PennFox Trackway's Wicked Brew has 13 all-breed Bests in show and has won the Breed at Montgomery. It should be noted that while the Westminster Kennel Club is the country's most prestigious all-breed show, Montgomery County Kennel Club is an equally prestigious show for terriers. Montgomery is the pinnacle of all-terrier shows, and Fox Terriers always have outstanding entries, with competitors coming from far

At the Westminster Kennel Club dog show, Ch. Cunning Fox Santeric Patriot won Best of Breed and Group 2. He is the sire of over 50 AKC champions. Owners, Kathy Reges and Ric Chashoudian.

Virginia Matanic, handling one of her lovely Wires to Group One.

and wide. A Best of Breed win at Montgomery is a wonderful win for a breeder of any terrier.

The Smooth Fox Terrier has not been alone in the ring, as his "brother," the Wire Fox Terrier, has become a very popular dog even though at the beginning he

BRITISH IMPORTS

Over the years a number of top British handlers have emigrated to the United States. Not only have these men (and they have almost all been men) handled the exceptional Fox Terriers of the century but they have also piloted numerous other terrier breeds to the Best in Show positions. Over the years their abilities and charm, along with their accents, have provided many formidable challenges for American handlers, but as the decades went on, the Americans have become a match for their British counterparts.

followed in the shadow of the Smooth Fox Terrier.

By the 1920s the Wire Fox Terriers were quickly gaining in popularity and there were many fine Wire kennels throughout the country. Up to the 1950s every decade saw at least one or more Wires winning the top spot at Westminster. The Smooth and Wire Fox Terriers won more Bests in Shows at Westminster than any other breed during the early decades of this show and still hold that distinction.

In the late 1920s Mr. and Mrs. Richard Bondy established the Wildoaks Kennels at Golden Bridge, NY. Between importing superior stock from England and the help of exceptional kennel management, they bred many superior Wires. The kennel was active for a good thirty years. In the late 1930s through the 1950s Mr. and Mrs. Thomas Carruthers III of Ohio established the Hetherington Kennels. Again, many homebred champions came from this kennel.

For three decades, from the 1940s through the 1960s, the Wire was popular and there were many breeders producing excellent specimens. Those particularly well known were Forrest Halle (Hallwyre Wires), Mrs. Paul M. Silvernail (Crack-Dale), Nick Calicura, Dr. John Masely and Thomas Gately (Gayterry), who all went on to become very popular

WESTMINSTER WINNERS

In the US, the Westminster Kennel Club show is the country's most prestigious show. It is held in New York City and is the oldest continuous dog show in the world. Although Westminster is 14 years older than the famous English Crufts Dog Show, it is a considerably smaller show, with only 2,500 dogs competing over two days. (Crufts enters over 20,000 dogs over four days.) Fox Terriers have been crowned the "Princes of Westminster," having won Best in Show there more than any other breed, a total of 17 times in the 20th century. Ch. Warren Remedy, a Smooth, won the first three Best in Show awards from 1907 through 1909. The following year another Smooth, Ch. Sabine Rarebit, took the honor. The torch was handed to the Wires as Ch. Matford Vic claimed Best in Show in 1915 and 1916, followed by another Wire in 1917, Ch. Conejo Wycollar Boy, who duplicated the feat again in 1920. The Wires continued with their victories: Ch. Signal Circuit of Halleston in 1926, Ch. Talavara Margaret in 1928, Ch. Pendley Calling of Blarney in 1930 and 1931, Ch. Flornell Spicy Bit of Halleston in 1934, Ch. Flornell Spicy Piece of Halleston in 1937, Ch. Heatherington Model Rhythm in 1946 and Ch. Zeloy Mooremaide's Magic in 1966. Ch. Registry's Lonesome Dove won the honor in 1992, the last Fox Terrier of the century to win Westminster.

dog show judges.

The 1970s was a very exciting decade for the Wires. Imported into the US was Eng. Ch. Sunnybrook Spot On, owned by Mrs. Robert Clark of Springfield Farms Kennels, handled by Peter Green. A huge winner and producer, Spot On really caught the public's eye. Following upon the heels of Spot On's arrival came another English dog, sired by Spot On, Ch. Aryee Dominator, owned by Michael Weissman and his mother. Dominator, handled by George Ward, became the top-winning Wire up to that time with 78 Bests in Show and 163 Group wins. These two dogs made a tremendous impact upon the breed.

Another well-known breeder, starting in the 1950s, was Eve Ballich, who bought her first bitch from the Bondys. Miss Ballich is still active in the breed and has produced over 100 champions. Ch. Evewire Druid Dynamic has produced nearly 30 champions, and Ch. Evewire You Better Believe It produced nearly 20 champions. Another top Wire breeder is Mari Morrisey. Her Brookhaven Kennels also has produced over 100 champions.

Starting in 1973, Virginia Matanic, Briarlea Kennels in Minnesota, bought her first dog and has finished no fewer than 55 homebred champions plus 15 champions that were bred by

The latest generation of the Kathrich and Santeric Wire Foxes, owned by Kathleen Reges and Ric Chashoudian. This is Ch. Kathrich Santeric Warpath.

others. Among Briarlea's top winners are Ch. Briarlea's Lancelot, Ch. Briarlea's Molly B at Redoaks, Ch. Briarlea's Vixen v Shadow Frost, Ch. Briarlea's DeJaVu and Ch. IABCA Best in Show, all of whom have won top awards in the US, Canada and beyond. What makes Ms. Matanic's record exceptional is that she has done all winning as an owner-handler, an impressive feat in any breed but especially difficult in a breed as competitive as the Wire Fox Terrier.

Finally, let's look at two of the great Wires of the century. In the late 1980s, there was the aptly named Ch. Galsul Excellence, owned by J. & William McKay and R. Cooper, who won 67 Best in Show awards, handled by master terrier man Peter Green. And, of course, who could forget Ch. Registry's Lonesome Dove? Known around the US as "Lacey," this flawless bitch won Best in Show at Westminster in 1992, expertly handled by Michael Kemp. Lacey, owned by Samuel and Marion Lawrence, won 120 Best in Show awards during her career.

In the early 1990s long-time handler and breeder Ric Chashoudian and Kathleen Reges of Santeric and Kathrich joined forces to do their best to produce great Wires. By using the best stud dogs from around the US and beyond, these two breeders have bred many top winners, in cooperation with other trusted breeders and their bitches. Among some of their great sires are Ch. Sylair Special Edition, the top Wire sire of all time with 90 champions; Ch. Sir John du Bois Des Maitres, top sire from Belgium; Ch. Cunning Fox Santeric Patriot, sire of 52 champions (and counting); and Ch. Starring Joint of Santeric, top sire from Finland. Among their many top winners are Ch. Kathrich Santeric Relentless, owned by Norm and Lynda Kenney with Kathleen Reges; Ch. Santeric Fleur de Lee, Montgomery winner 2003; Ch. Kathrich Santeric Windfall and Ch. Santeric 4 Two K of Kathrich.

FOX TERRIERS AROUND THE WORLD

Fox Terriers have been known for decades in Canada, the first one being registered in 1887. James D. Strachar from Montreal founded the famous Ormandy Kennels in 1919. Mr. and Mrs. Frank Beers from Toronto were well known in

Smooths in the 1930s and 1940s. Albany Kennels of Ted Ward, Sr. were also well known and his son George Ward, who moved to the United States, is a very well-known terrier handler, piloting many famous Wires as well as West Highland White Terriers to the top spots at the best of American shows.

Fox Terriers have been in Australia for over a century, with the first Smooth imported from England in 1868. This bitch, Careless, formed the foundation for the breed in that country. The first Wire imported from England was Nell, imported in 1876. Canbury Fox Terriers, owned by Barbara Withen, was started in 1966 with an English champion. Her kennel has been very successful with Group winners and Best in Show winners. Her Ch. Pende Pied Piper won 54 Bests in Show. Many dogs of her breeding have been exported to the United States. The breed in Australia is popular and in very good hands!

Fox Terriers, unlike many other breeds, have made their mark throughout the world, from Brazil to Denmark to Japan. In Italy, Ch. Seawire Silver Bell was the winner of three Bests in Show. In Japan, Ch. Townville Tarique won four all-breed Bests in Show before he was returned to England. In Norway, where the breed has been established since 1893, one of the most recent winners was Ch.

Ch. Sylair Special Edition, the top Wire sire of all time. He produced 90 AKC champions.

Louline Heartbreaker, winner of 5 Bests in Show and 11 Group firsts in 16 outings.

The Fox Terrier, now in its second century, has become a popular breed throughout the world. This smart dog continues to be a top winner and certainly is a beloved pet wherever he resides. England continues to be its home, but top dogs are now coming from many countries around the world. The Fox Terrier, Smooth and Wire, is in good hands from North America to the Continent, to Australia and to the Far East.

Ch. Jenwyres George Cinq of Santeric, owned by Ric Chashoudian and Kathy Reges, was a top winner in Japan and won Best of Breed at Westminster Kennel Club dog show in 2000. Here's he's taking a Best in Show at a Japan Kennel Club dog show.

CHARACTERISTICS OF THE

FOX TERRIER

IS THE FOX TERRIER THE DOG FOR YOU?

The Fox Terrier is a stylish, lively dog—he is full of spirit, he is intelligent, he is game and he is every inch a terrier. He is smart and attractive, possessing unfailing optimism and unquestioning courage. He is a handsome dog to behold, desirable as a canine pal and all-around pet. In addition, he is a nice-sized dog, easy to have in an apartment in the city. However, he is a very active dog and likes to have a master who is as equally interested in life as he is.

A common characteristic of all terriers is their desire to work with great enthusiasm and courage. They all have large and powerful teeth for the size of their bodies, as well as keen hearing and excellent eyesight. No matter for how many generations they have been bred as pets, the purpose for which the breed was created will remain in the dog.

The active Fox Terrier is not the breed for someone who is looking for the sedentary lap dog. I grew up with a Wire Fox Terrier who was rambunctious throughout his puppyhood, which lasted until the age of 12. I later had many other terriers who were always ready to chase a squirrel or go after a rabbit. These dogs are far too busy to sit on a lap.

If you like the spirit of a Fox Terrier, you will find that they are a wonderful size for a household companion, being no taller than 15.5 inches and weighing around 18 pounds for a male and several pounds less for a female. The Smooth requires little grooming, but the Wire will require grooming whether he is a pet or a show dog. The Fox Terrier's intelligence can sometimes be like a double-edged sword: quick to learn and sometimes quick to get bored. They immediately can work out what is expected of them and are just as quick to work their way around your expectations.

Fox Terriers are basically no-nonsense dogs. They will not stand in the yard and bark for hours as some breeds will, but they will bark when they hear a noise and want to alert their owners. They are natural-born fighters and will enjoy a scrap on occasion, or at least enjoy the thrill of chasing a cat up a tree. All terriers, given their inbred instincts, have a tendency to dig in the garden if they are bored.

It must be determined early on who is going to be the boss of the household but, because of their intelligence, they are easy to

DELTA SOCIETY

The human-animal bond propels the work of the Delta Society, striving to improve the lives of people and animals. The Pet Partners Program proves that the lives of people and dogs are inextricably linked. The Pet Partners Program, a national registry, trains and screens volunteers for pet therapy in hospices, nursing homes, schools and rehabilitation centers. Dog-and-handler teams of Pet Partners volunteer in all 50 states, with nearly 7,000 teams making visits annually. About 900,000 patients, residents and students receive assistance each year. If you and your dog are interested in becoming Pet Partners, contact the Delta Society online at www.deltasociety.org.

train and easy to live with. They make wonderful household pets who thoroughly enjoy their family and their activities. These days they are more at home sitting on a sofa near the fireplace than out on the moors chasing the fox.

If you are a first-time dog owner you must be aware of your responsibility toward your new friend. Keep your dog either on a leash when out on a walk or in your fenced yard. Your Fox Terrier, if loose and trotting along at your side, will spot a squirrel across a busy street and his instincts will have him darting across the street, oblivious of the traffic. Therefore, some rudimentary obedience training should be in line so your pal will sit when asked to, come when called and in general act like a little gentleman.

Fox Terriers, as with other terriers, can be a challenge in the obedience ring. Terriers are not an easy breed to work with in obedience. Their above-average

intelligence and independent spirit can sometimes be more trying to the trainer than anticipated. You will see Golden Retrievers, Poodles and Shetland Sheepdogs in abundance in obedience classes, as these are breeds that are easy to work with. Not only are they intelligent, but more importantly, they have a willingness to please their masters. The terrier is easily distracted and busy, but he is an intelligent dog and he does respond to training. Of course, when training a smart and independent dog, the handler will often learn humility while the dog is learning his "sits" and "stays." The Fox Terrier is a quick, alert and intelligent dog, and he likes his owner to be his equal.

BREED-SPECIFIC HEALTH CONSIDERATIONS

Fox Terriers are very healthy dogs, as are most terriers. However, there are health problems in most breeds of dog and the Fox Terrier

If there is such a thing as an ideal dog for children, the Fox Terrier would have to be it.

Fox Terriers need exercise on a daily basis. If you are unable to handle this routine, you might be better off with a less demanding breed.

is no exception. The new owner should be aware of these problems before buying his dog. Do remember to buy your puppy from a reputable breeder and ask the breeder if any of these health problems are in his line.

LENS LUXATION AND CATARACTS
Subluxation is a slightly altered position of the lens and luxation is total lens displacement. Trauma, inheritance, glaucoma and, of course, aging all contribute to the loss or rupture of the sonular attachments between the lens and ciliary body. A luxated lens is painful and the eye will be red and opaque. Vision is saved with prompt removal of the lens and the dog will be on ocular medication for his lifetime. There

is an inherited predisposition to lens luxation. Subluxations can usually be managed with medication by controlling the inflammation. Cataracts are common in all older dogs. An opacity in the lens will be noted and there will be some degree of vision impairment that increases as the dog ages.

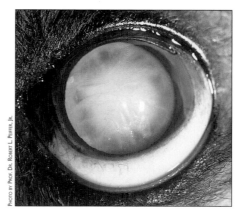

PHOTO BY PROF. DR. ROBERT L. PEIFFER, JR.

Anterior lens luxation can occur as a primary disease in Fox Terriers, or secondarily after an accident. The fibers that hold the lens in place rupture and the lens may migrate through the pupil to be situated in front of the iris.

Because they are such active dogs, Fox Terriers often have shoulder dislocations. These are usually successfully treated by your veterinarian

ATOPIC DERMATITIS

This is an allergy-related skin problem that can be inherited. In the dog, allergies will usually show up as skin lesions. Your veterinarian should assist with the identification or cause of the allergy, and then he will recommend therapeutic intervention, usually in the form of baths with medicated soap or topical ointments.

OTHER PROBLEMS

In addition to those previously mentioned, Fox Terriers will have problems with shoulder dislocations, and a rare few have problems with Legg-Perthes disease. However, the Fox Terrier is considered to be a healthy breed; these potential problems are mentioned only so that a buyer will be aware of them. If the breeder of your puppy is reputable and aware of these problems, he will be doing

his utmost to keep them out of his line.

William Haynes wrote in 1925, "The terrier owner is a 'lucky devil' for his dogs do not, as a rule, spend a great deal of time in hospital. All members of the terrier family, from the giant of the race, the Airedale, way down to little Scottie, owe a big debt to Nature for having blessed them with remarkably robust constitutions. Even when really sick, they make wonderfully rapid recoveries."

SKIN PROBLEMS

Eczema and dermatitis are skin problems that occur in many breeds; they can often be a tricky problem to solve. Frequent bathing of the dog will remove skin oils and will cause the problem to worsen. Allergies to food or something in the environment can also cause the problem. Consider trying homeopathic remedies in addition to seeing your veterinarian for direction.

Not only are Fox Terriers great fun but they often come decorated like clowns!

FOX TERRIER

Each breed approved by the American Kennel Club (AKC) has a standard that gives the reader a mental picture of what that breed should look like. All reputable breeders strive to produce animals that will meet the requirements of the standard. Many breeds were developed for a specific purpose, i.e., hunting, retrieving, going to ground, coursing, guarding, herding and so on. The terriers were all bred to go to ground and to pursue vermin.

In addition to having dogs that look like a correct Fox Terrier, the standard assures that the dog will have the personality, disposition and intelligence that is sought after in the breed.

Standards were originally written by fanciers who had a love and a concern for the breed, as well as a knowledge of basic animal structure, as many early Fox Terrier enthusiasts were also educated horse folk. They knew that the essential characteristics of the Fox Terrier were unlike any other breed and that care must be taken that these characteristics were maintained through the generations.

As time progressed, breeders became more aware that certain areas of the dog needed a better description or more definition, as many new dog fanciers did not have a thorough knowledge of basic mammalian structure. Knowledgeable breeders would meet together and work out a new standard, which included a more complete portrait of the whole

Exhibits at a conformation show are compared to the breed standard, the written description of the perfect breed specimen. The dog that most closely conforms to the standard is selected as the Best of Breed winner.

animal. Today standards for any breed are never changed on a whim, and serious study and exchange between breeders take place before any alteration is made. American Kennel Club breed standards have been intact for many years, despite some reformatting and minor word changes.

Now let's take a look at the two breed standards for the Smooth and Wire Fox Terriers. The versions presented here have been abbreviated, excluding any repetitive wordage from one standard to the other. For the complete standards, visit the AKC's website.

AKC BREED STANDARD FOR THE SMOOTH FOX TERRIER
General Appearance: The dog must present a generally gay, lively and active appearance; bone and strength in a small compass are essentials; but this must not be taken to mean that a Fox Terrier should be cloddy, or in any way coarse—speed and endurance must be looked to as well as power, and the symmetry of the Foxhound taken as a model. The Terrier, like the Hound, must on no account be leggy, nor must he be too short in the leg. He should stand like a cleverly made hunter, covering a lot of ground, yet with

The Smooth Fox Terrier must be neither too short on leg nor leggy, though he must cover a lot of ground. Like the Wire, the Smooth has a short back, a key element of the breed's construction.

On the Smooth's head, there is no noticeable difference in length between the skull, which should be flat and moderately narrow, and the foreface. The stop is hardly noticeable though it is more apparent than that of a Greyhound

a short back, as stated below. He will then attain the highest degree of propelling power, together with the greatest length of stride that is compatible with the length of his body. Weight is not a certain criterion of a Terrier's fitness for his work—general shape, size and contour are the main points; and if a dog can gallop and stay, and follow his fox up a drain, it matters little what his weight is to a pound or so.

N.B. Old scars or injuries, the result of work or accident, should not be allowed to prejudice a Terrier's chance in the show ring, unless they interfere with its movement or with its utility for work or stud.

Size, Proportion, Substance:
According to present-day requirements, a full-sized, well balanced dog should not exceed 15.5 inches at the withers—the bitch being proportionately lower—nor should the length of back from withers to root of tail exceed 12 inches, while to maintain the relative proportions, the head should not exceed 7.5 inches or be less than 7 inches. A dog with these measurements should scale 18 pounds in show condition—a bitch weighing some two pounds less—with a margin of one pound either way. *Balance*—This may be defined as the correct proportions of a certain point, or points, when considered in relation to a certain other point or points. It is the keystone of the Terrier's anatomy.

Head: Eyes and rims should be dark in color, moderately small and rather deep set, full of fire, life and intelligence and as nearly possible circular in shape. Anything approaching a yellow eye is most objectionable. Ears should be V-shaped and small, of moderate thickness, and dropping forward close to the cheek, not hanging by the side of the head like a Foxhound. The topline of the folded ear should be well above the level of the skull. *Disqualifications*—Ears prick, tulip or rose.

The skull should be flat and moderately narrow, gradually decreasing in width to the eyes. Not much "stop" should be apparent, but there should be more dip in the profile between the forehead and the top jaw than is seen in the case of a Greyhound. There should be apparent little difference in length between the skull and foreface of a well balanced head. Cheeks must not be full.

Jaws, upper and lower, should be strong and muscular and of fair punishing strength, but not so as in any way to resemble the Greyhound or modern English Terrier. There should not be much falling away below the eyes. This part of the head should, however, be moderately chiseled out, so as not to go down in a straight slope like a wedge. The nose, toward which the muzzle must gradually taper, should be black. *Disqualifications*—Nose white, cherry or spotted to a considerable extent with either of these colors.

The teeth should be as nearly as possible together, i.e., the points of the upper (incisors) teeth on the outside of or slightly overlapping the lower teeth. *Disqualifications*—Much undershot, or much overshot.

Neck, Topline, Body: Neck should be clean and muscular, without throatiness, of fair length, and gradually widening to the shoulders. Back should be short, straight (i.e., level), and strong, with no appearance of slackness.

Chest deep and not broad. Brisket should be deep, yet not exaggerated. The foreribs should be moderately arched, the back ribs deep and well sprung, and the dog should be well ribbed up. Loin should be very powerful, muscular and very slightly arched. Stern should be set on rather high, and carried gaily, but not over the back or curled, docked to leave about three quarters of the original length of the tail.

Forequarters: Shoulders should be long and sloping, well laid back, fine at the points, and clearly cut at the withers. The elbows should hang perpendicular to the body, working free of the sides. The forelegs viewed from any direction must be straight with bone strong right down to the feet, showing little or no appearance of ankle in front, and being short and straight in pastern. Both fore and hind legs should be carried straight forward in traveling. Feet should be round, compact, and not large; the soles hard and tough; the toes moderately arched, and turned neither in nor out.

Hindquarters: Should be strong and muscular, quite free from droop or crouch; the thighs long and powerful, stifles well curved and turned neither in nor out; hocks well bent and near the ground should be perfectly upright and parallel each with the other when viewed from behind, the dog standing well up on them like a Foxhound, and not straight in the stifle. Both fore and hind legs should be carried straight forward in traveling, the stifles not turning outward. Feet as in front.

Coat: Should be smooth, flat, but hard, dense and abundant. The belly and underside of the thighs should not be bare.

Color: White should predominate; brindle, red or liver markings are objectionable. Otherwise this point is of little or no importance.

The topline of the skull should be almost flat. The nose must be black.

Gait: The Terrier's legs should be carried straight forward while traveling, the forelegs hanging perpendicular and swinging parallel with the sides, like the pendulum of a clock. The principal propulsive power is furnished by the hind legs, perfection of action being found in the Terrier possessing long thighs and muscular second thighs well bent at the stifles, which admit of a strong forward thrust or "snatch" of the hocks.

Temperament: The dog must present a generally gay, lively and active appearance.

Approved July 8, 2002
Effective August 28, 2002

AKC BREED STANDARD FOR THE WIRE FOX TERRIER
General Appearance: The Terrier should be alert, quick of movement, keen of expression, on the tip-toe of expectation at the slightest provocation. Character is imparted by the expression of the eyes and by the carriage of ears and tail.

Bone and strength in a small compass are essential, but this must not be taken to mean that a Terrier should be "cloddy," or in any way coarse—speed and endurance being requisite as well

as power. The Terrier must on no account be leggy, nor must he be too short on the leg. He should stand like a cleverly made, short-backed hunter, covering a lot of ground.

Head: The length of the head of a full-grown well developed dog of correct size—measured with calipers—from the back of the occipital bone to the nostrils—should be from 7 to 7.25 inches, the bitch's head being proportionately shorter. In a well balanced head there should be little apparent difference in length between skull and foreface.

Keen of expression. Eyes should be dark in color, moderately small, rather deep-set, not prominent, and full of fire, life, and intelligence; as nearly as possible circular in shape, and not too far apart. Anything approaching a yellow eye is most objectionable. Ears should be small and V-shaped and of moderate thickness, the flaps neatly folded over and dropping forward close to the cheeks. *Disqualifications*—Ears prick, tulip or rose.

The topline of the skull should be almost flat, sloping slightly and gradually decreasing in width toward the eyes, and should not exceed 3.5 inches in diameter at the widest part—measuring with the calipers—in the full-grown dog of correct size,

the bitch's skull being proportionately narrower.

Nose should be black. *Disqualifications*—Nose white, cherry or spotted to a considerable extent with either of these colors. *Mouth*—Both upper and lower jaws should be strong and muscular, the teeth as nearly as possible level and capable of closing together like a vise—the lower canines locking in front of the upper and the points of the upper incisors slightly overlapping the lower. *Disqualifications*—Much undershot, or much overshot.

Neck, Topline, Body: Neck should be clean, muscular, of fair length, free from throatiness and presenting a graceful curve when viewed from the side. The back should be short and level with no appearance of slackness—the

"A cleverly made, short-backed hunter" well describes the Wire Fox Terrier, who must be strong and well boned but never cloddy. This is a terrier built for movement as well as power.

loins muscular and very slightly arched. The bitch may be slightly longer in couplings than the dog.

Chest deep and not broad, a too narrow chest being almost as undesirable as a very broad one. Excessive depth of chest and brisket is an impediment to a Terrier when going to ground. The brisket should be deep, the front ribs moderately arched, and the back ribs deep and well sprung. Tail should be set on rather high and carried gaily but not curled. It should be of good strength and substance and of fair length—a three-quarters dock is about right—since it affords the only safe grip when handling working Terriers.

Forequarters: Shoulders when viewed from the front should slope steeply downwards from their juncture, with the neck towards the points, which should be fine. When viewed from the side they should be long, well laid back, and should slope obliquely backwards from points to withers, which should always be clean-cut. The elbows should hang perpendicular to the body, working free of the sides, carried straight through in traveling. Viewed from any direction the legs should be straight, the bone of the forelegs strong right down to the feet. Feet should be round, compact, and not large—the pads tough and well cushioned, and the toes moderately arched and turned neither in nor out.

Coat: The best coats appear to be broken, the hairs having a tendency to twist, and are of dense, wiry texture—like coconut matting—the hairs growing so closely and strongly together that, when parted with the fingers, the skin cannot be seen. At the base of these stiff hairs is a shorter growth of finer and softer hair—termed the undercoat. The coat on the sides is never quite so hard as that on the back and quarters. Some of the hardest coats are "crinkly" or slightly waved, but a curly coat is very objectionable. The hair on the upper and lower jaws should be crisp and only sufficiently long to impart an appearance of strength to the foreface. The hair on the forelegs should also be dense and crisp. The coat should average in length from .75 to 1 inch on shoulders and neck, lengthening to 1.5 inches on withers, back, ribs, and quarters.

Temperament: The Terrier should be alert, quick of movement, keen of expression, on the tip-toe of expectation at the slightest provocation.

Approved February 9, 1991
Effective March 27, 1991

Correct ear placement.

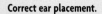

WIRE

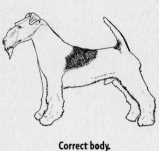

Correct body.

SMOOTH

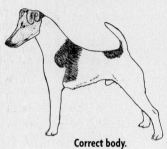

Correct body.

Incorrect: rose ears.

Incorrect: body too long; weak pasterns.

Low-set tail; over-angulated hock.

Correct tail.

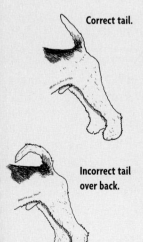

Incorrect tail over back.

Correct: straight front legs.

Incorrect: front feet turning outward.

Correct: straight front legs.

Incorrect: legs bowing inward.

FOX TERRIER

WHERE TO BEGIN

If you are convinced that the Fox Terrier is the ideal dog for you, it's time to learn about where to find a puppy and what to look for. Locating a litter of Fox Terriers, whether Smooth or Wire, should not present a problem for the new owner. You should inquire about breeders in your area who have earned a good reputation in the breed. You are looking for an established breeder with outstanding dog ethics, success in the show ring and a strong commitment to the breed.

New owners should have as many questions as they have doubts. An established breeder is indeed the one to answer your many questions and make you comfortable with your choice of the Fox Terrier. An established breeder will sell you a puppy at a fair price if, and only if, the breeder determines that you are a suitable, worthy owner of his/her dogs. An established breeder can be relied upon for advice at any reasonable time. A reputable breeder will accept a puppy back, often without penalty, should you decide that this is not the right dog for you. When choosing a breeder, reputation is much more important than convenience of location.

Choosing a breeder is an important first step in dog ownership. Fortunately, the majority of Fox Terrier breeders are devoted to the breed and its well-being. New owners should have little problem finding a reputable breeder who doesn't live in another state or on the other side of the country (or in a different country). The American Kennel Club is able to recommend breeders of quality Fox Terriers, as can any local all-breed club or Fox Terrier club. Potential owners are encouraged to attend a dog show to see the Fox Terriers in action, to meet the handlers firsthand and to get an idea what quality Fox Terriers look like outside a photographer's lens. Provided you approach the owners when they are not too terribly busy with the dogs, most will be more than willing to answer questions, recommend breeders and give advice.

Now that you have contacted and met a breeder or two and made your choice about which breeder is best suited to your needs, it's time to visit the litter. Keep in mind that many top

When selecting a Fox Terrier puppy, Smooth or Wire, it's imperative to meet the dam (and sire, if possible), so that you can assess how your puppy will develop as an adult.

MAKE A COMMITMENT

Dogs are most assuredly man's best friend, but they are also a lot of work. When you add a puppy to your family, you also are adding to your daily responsibilities for years to come. Dogs need more than just food, water and a place to sleep. They also require training (which can be ongoing throughout the lifetime of the dog), activity to keep them physically and mentally fit and hands-on attention every day, plus grooming and health care. Your life as you now know it may well disappear! Are you prepared for such drastic changes?

Since you are likely choosing a Fox Terrier as a pet dog and not a show dog, you should simply select a pup that is friendly and appealing. Fox Terriers generally have small litters, averaging five puppies, so selection is somewhat limited once you have located a desirable litter. While the basic structure of the breed has little variation, beware of the shy or overly aggressive puppy: be especially conscious of the nervous Fox Terrier pup. Don't let sentiment or emotion trap you into buying the runt of the litter.

The sex of your puppy is largely a matter of personal taste; many owners feel that males are more loyal, but females are more affectionate. With a bitch, the owner must contend with the semiannual estrous cycles (which can be difficult to handle). Males may wander away from home in pursuit of a bitch in heat, but this is not a major factor since most pet owners have their Fox Terriers neutered. As any veterinarian will attest, neutering the bitch and the dog reaps many health benefits and also calms the animal down temperamentally.

The choice of which coat type the owner prefers—in the case of Fox Terriers, it's really the choice of a breed—is also a matter of personal taste and time commitment. Some owners prefer the sleek appearance of the Smooth, happily accompanied by an easy-

breeders have waiting lists. Sometimes new owners have to wait as long as two years for a puppy. If you are really committed to the breeder whom you've selected, then you will wait for one of his puppies, or perhaps he can recommend another breeder who has his bloodline.

care coat and loving ways. Others seek out the distinctive appearance of the Wire and do not mind the extra care the wire coat requires to keep looking its best. Even a Wire Fox Terrier kept in a "pet clip" requires significant maintenance.

Breeders commonly allow visitors to see the litter by around the fifth or sixth week, and puppies leave for their new homes between the eighth and tenth week. Breeders who permit their puppies to leave earlier are more interested in your money than their puppies' well-being. Puppies need to learn the rules of the trade from their dams, and most dams continue teaching the pups manners, and dos and don'ts, until around the eighth week. Breeders spend significant amounts of time with the Fox Terrier toddlers so that they are able to interact with the "other species," i.e., humans. Given the long history that dogs and humans have, bonding between the two species is natural but must be nurtured.

A COMMITTED NEW OWNER

By now you should understand what makes the Fox Terrier a most unique and special dog, one that may fit nicely into your family and lifestyle. If you have researched breeders, you should be able to recognize a knowledge-able and responsible Fox Terrier

SELECTING FROM THE LITTER

Before you visit a litter of puppies, promise yourself that you won't fall for the first pretty face you see! Decide on your goals for your puppy—show prospect, hunting dog, obedience competitor, family companion—and then look for a puppy who displays the appropriate qualities. In most litters, there is an Alpha pup (the bossy puppy), and occasionally a shy fellow who is less confident, with the rest of the litter falling somewhere in the middle. "Middle-of-the-roaders" are safe bets for most families and novice competitors.

breeder who cares not only about his pups but also about what kind of owner you will be. If you have completed the final step in your

FINDING A QUALIFIED BREEDER

Before you begin your puppy search, ask for references from your veterinarian and perhaps other breeders to refer you to someone they believe is reputable. Responsible breeders usually raise only one or two breeds of dog. Avoid any breeder who has several different breeds or has several litters at the same time. Dedicated breeders are usually involved with a breed or other dog club. Many participate in some sport or activity related to their breed. Just as you want to be assured of the breeder's qualifications, the breeder wants to be assured that you will make a worthy owner. Expect the breeder to interview you, asking questions about your goals for the pup, your experience with dogs and what kind of home you will provide.

new journey, you have found a litter, or possibly two, of quality Fox Terrier pups.

A visit with the puppies and their breeder should be an education in itself. Breed research, breeder selection and puppy visitation are very important aspects of finding the puppy of your dreams. Beyond that, these things also lay the foundation for a successful future with your pup. Puppy personalities within each litter vary, from the shy and easygoing puppy to the one who is dominant and assertive, with most pups falling somewhere in between. By spending time with the puppies you will be able to recognize certain behaviors and what these behaviors indicate about each pup's temperament. Which type of pup will complement your family dynamics is best determined by observing the puppies in action within their "pack." Your breeder's expertise and recommendations are also valuable. Although you may fall in love with a bold and brassy male, the breeder may suggest that another pup would be best for you. The breeder's experience in rearing Fox Terrier pups and matching their temperaments with appropriate humans offers the best assurance that your pup will meet your needs and expectations. The type of puppy that you select is just as important as your decision that the Fox Terrier is the breed for you.

The decision to live with a Fox Terrier is a serious commitment and not one to be taken lightly. This puppy is a living sentient being that will be dependent on you for basic survival for his entire life.

Sometimes it's difficult to narrow down your selection to the one pup that's meant for you. If you've found a qualified, caring breeder, trust his advice in making your final choice.

PEDIGREE VS. REGISTRATION CERTIFICATE

Too often new owners are confused between these two important documents. Your puppy's pedigree, essentially a family tree, is a written record of a dog's genealogy of three generations or more. The pedigree will show you the names as well as performance titles of all dogs in your pup's background. Your breeder must provide you with a registration application, with his part properly filled out. You must complete the application and send it to the AKC with the proper fee. Every puppy must come from a litter that has been AKC-registered by the breeder, born in the US and from a sire and dam that are also registered with the AKC.

The seller must provide you with complete records to identify the puppy. The AKC requires that the seller provide the buyer with the following: breed; sex, color and markings; date of birth; litter number (when available); names and registration numbers of the parents; breeder's name; and date sold or delivered.

Beyond the basics of survival—food, water, shelter and protection—he needs much, much more. The new pup needs love, nurturing and a proper canine education to mold him into a responsible, well-behaved canine citizen. Your Fox Terrier's health and good manners will need consistent monitoring and regular "tune-ups," so your job as a responsible dog owner will be ongoing throughout every stage of his life. If you are not prepared to accept these responsibilities and commit to them for the next decade, likely longer, then you are not prepared to own a dog of any breed.

Although the responsibilities of owning a dog may at times tax your patience, the joy of living with your Fox Terrier far outweighs the workload, and a well-mannered adult dog is worth your time and effort. Before your very eyes, your new charge will grow up to be your most loyal friend, devoted to you unconditionally.

SOME DAM ATTITUDE

When selecting a puppy, be certain to meet the dam of the litter. The temperament of the dam is often predictive of the temperament of her puppies. However, dams occasionally are very protective of their young, some to the point of being testy or aggressive with visitors, whom they may view as a danger to their babies. Such attitudes are more common when the pups are very young and still nursing and should not be mistaken for actual aggressive temperament. If possible, visit the dam away from her pups to make friends with her and gain a better understanding of her true personality.

YOUR FOX TERRIER SHOPPING LIST

Just as expectant parents prepare a nursery for their baby, so should you ready your home for the arrival of your Fox Terrier pup. If you have the necessary puppy supplies purchased and in place before he comes home, it will ease the puppy's transition from the warmth and familiarity of his mom and littermates to the brand-new environment of his new home and human family. You will be too busy to stock up and prepare your house after your pup comes home, that's for sure! Imagine how a pup must feel upon being transported to a strange new place. It's up to you to comfort him and to let your little pup know that he is going to be happy with you.

FOOD AND WATER BOWLS

Your puppy will need separate bowls for his food and water. Stainless steel bowls are generally preferred over plastic bowls since they sterilize better and pups are less inclined to chew on the metal. Heavy-duty ceramic bowls are popular, but consider how often you will have to pick up those heavy bowls. Buy adult-sized bowls, as your puppy will grow into them in no time.

THE DOG CRATE

If you think that crates are tools of punishment and confinement

SIGNS OF A HEALTHY PUPPY
Healthy puppies are robust little fellows who are alert and active, sporting shiny coats and supple skin. They should not appear lethargic, bloated or pot-bellied, nor should they have flaky skin or runny or crusted eyes or noses. Their stools should be firm and well formed, with no evidence of blood or mucus.

for when a dog has misbehaved, think again. Most breeders and almost all trainers recommend a crate as the preferred house-training aid as well as for all-around puppy training and safety. Because dogs are natural den creatures that prefer cave-like environments, the benefits of crate use are many. The crate provides the puppy with his very own "safe house," a cozy place to sleep, take a break or seek comfort with a favorite toy; a travel aid to house your dog when on the road, at motels or at the vet's office; a training aid to help teach your puppy proper toileting habits; a place of solitude when non-dog people

happen to drop by and don't want a lively puppy—or even a well-behaved adult dog—saying hello or begging for attention.

Crates come in several types, although the wire crate and the fiberglass airline-type crate are the most popular. Both are safe and your puppy will adjust to either one, so the choice is up to you. The wire crates offer better visibility for the pup as well as better ventilation. Many of the wire crates easily collapse into suitcase-size carriers. The fiberglass crates, similar to those used by the airlines for animal transport, are sturdier and more den-like. However, the fiberglass crates do not collapse and are less ventilated than a wire crate, which can be problematic in hot weather. Some of the newer crates are made of heavy plastic mesh; they are very lightweight and fold up into slim-line suitcases. However, a mesh crate might not

Be prepared for your puppy's arrival by having the right feeding vessels for him. Most breeders recommend stainless steel bowls, though your puppy won't care too much as long as there's good kibble and fresh water inside them.

Along with the expenses, inconvieniences and messes, your new Fox Terrier puppy brings joy.

be suitable for a pup with manic chewing habits.

Don't bother with a puppy-sized crate. Although your Fox Terrier will be a small fellow when you bring him home, he will grow up in the blink of an eye and your puppy crate will be useless. Purchase a crate that will accommodate an adult Fox Terrier. He will stand about 15 inches when full grown, so a medium-sized crate will fit him nicely.

BEDDING AND CRATE PADS
Your puppy will enjoy some type of soft bedding in his "room" (the crate), something he can snuggle into to feel cozy and secure. Old towels or blankets are good choices for a young pup, since he may (and probably will) have a toileting accident or two in the crate or decide to chew on the bedding material. Once he is fully trained and out of the early chewing stage, you can replace the puppy bedding with a permanent crate pad if you prefer. Crate pads and other dog beds run the gamut from inexpensive to high-end doggie-designer styles, but don't splurge on the good stuff until you are sure that your puppy is reliable and won't tear it up or make a mess on it.

ROCK-A-BYE BEDDING
The wide assortment of dog beds today can make your choice quite difficult, as there are many adorable novelty beds in fun styles and prints. It's wise to wait until your puppy has outgrown the chewing stage before providing him with a dog bed, since he might make confetti out of it. Your puppy will be happy with an old towel or blanket in his crate until he is old enough to resist the temptation to chew up his bed. For a dog of any age, a bed with a washable cover is always a wise choice.

A small travel crate won't last very long for your growing Fox Terrier pup. Your wisest investment will be a medium-sized wire crate, which should last for the lifetime of the dog.

PUPPY TOYS
Just as infants and older children require objects to stimulate their minds and bodies, puppies need toys to entertain their curious brains, wiggly paws and achy teeth. A fun array of safe doggie

toys will help satisfy your puppy's chewing instincts and distract him from gnawing on the leg of your antique chair or your new leather sofa. Most puppy toys are cute and look as if they would be a lot of fun, but not all are necessarily safe or good for your puppy, so use caution when you go puppy-toy shopping.

Although Fox Terriers are not known to be voracious chewers like many other dogs, they still love to chew. The best "chewcifiers" are nylon and hard rubber bones, which are safe to gnaw on and come in sizes appropriate for all age groups and breeds. Be especially careful of natural bones, which can splinter or develop dangerous sharp edges;

pups can easily swallow or choke on those bone splinters. Veterinarians often tell of surgical nightmares involving bits of splintered bone, because in addition to the danger of choking, the sharp pieces can damage the intestinal tract.

Similarly, rawhide chews, while a favorite of most dogs and puppies, can be equally dangerous. Pieces of rawhide are easily swallowed after they get all gummy from chewing, and dogs have been known to choke on large pieces of ingested rawhide. Rawhide chews should be offered only when you can supervise the puppy.

Soft woolly toys are special puppy favorites. They come in a

Wire Foxes can be "wired," having lots of energy and enthusiasm for life. Providing safe interactive chew toys for your puppy will help to defuse some of his electric energy.

wide variety of cute shapes and sizes; some look like little stuffed animals. Puppies love to shake them up and toss them about, or simply carry them around. Be careful of fuzzy toys that have button eyes or noses that your pup could chew off and swallow, and make sure that he does not disembowel a squeaky toy to remove the squeaker! Braided rope toys are similar in that they are fun to chew and toss around, but they shred easily and the strings are easy to swallow. The strings are not digestible and, if the puppy doesn't pass them in his stool, he could end up at the vet's office. As with rawhides, your puppy should be closely monitored with rope toys.

If you believe that your pup has ingested one of these forbidden objects, check his stools for the next couple of days to see if he passes them when he defecates. At the same time, also watch for signs of intestinal distress. A call to your veterinarian might be in order to get his advice and be on the safe side.

An all-time favorite toy for puppies (young and old!) is the empty gallon milk jug. Hard plastic juice containers—46 ounces or more—are also excellent. Such containers make lots of noise when they are batted about, and puppies go crazy with delight as they play with them. However, they don't often last

TOYS 'R SAFE

The vast array of tantalizing puppy toys is staggering. Stroll through any pet shop or pet-supply outlet and you will see that the choices can be overwhelming. However, not all dog toys are safe or sensible. Most very young puppies enjoy soft woolly toys that they can snuggle with and carry around. (You know they have outgrown them when they shred them up!) Avoid toys that have buttons, tabs or other enhancements that can be chewed off and swallowed. Soft toys that squeak are fun, but make sure your puppy does not disembowel the toy and remove (and swallow) the squeaker. Toys that rattle or make noise can excite a puppy, but they present the same danger as the squeaky kind and so require supervision. Hard rubber toys that bounce can also entertain a pup, but make sure that the toy is too big for your pup to swallow.

COLLARING OUR CANINES

The standard flat collar with a buckle or a snap, in leather, nylon or cotton, is widely regarded as the everyday all-purpose collar. If the collar fits correctly, you should be able to fit two fingers between the collar and the dog's neck.

Leather Buckle Collars

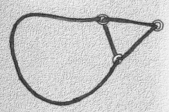

Limited-Slip Collar

The martingale, Greyhound or limited-slip collar is preferred by many dog owners and trainers. It is fixed with an extra loop that tightens when pressure is applied to the leash. The martingale collar gets tighter but does not "choke" the dog. The limited-slip collar should only be used for walking and training, not for free play or interaction with another dog. These types of collar should never be left on the dog, as the extra loop can lead to accidents.

Choke collars, usually made of stainless steel, are made for training purposes but are not recommended for small dogs or heavily coated breeds. The chains can injure small dogs or damage long/abundant coats. Thin nylon choke leads are commonly used on show dogs while in the ring, though they are not practical for everyday use.

Snap Bolt Choke Collar

The harness, with two or three straps that attach over the dog's shoulders and around his torso, is a humane and safe alternative to the conventional collar. By and large, a well-made harness is virtually escape-proof. Harnesses are available in nylon and mesh and can be outfitted on most dogs, ranging from chest girths of 10 to 30 inches.

Harness

Nylon Collar

Quick-Click Closure

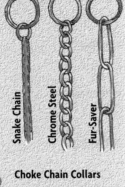

Snake Chain **Chrome Steel** **Fur-Saver**

Choke Chain Collars

A head collar, composed of a nylon strap that goes around the dog's muzzle and a second strap that wraps around his neck, offers the owner better control over his dog. This device is recommended for problem-solving with dogs (including jumping up, pulling and aggressive behaviors), but must be used with care.

A training halter, including a flat collar and two straps, made of nylon and webbing, is designed for walking. There are several on the market; some are more difficult to put on the dog than others. The halter harness, with two small slip rings at each end, is recommended for ease of use.

very long, so be sure to remove and replace them when they get chewed up on the ends.

A word of caution about homemade toys: be careful with your choices of non-traditional play objects. Never use old shoes or socks, since a puppy cannot distinguish between the old ones on which he's allowed to chew and the new ones in your closet that are strictly off limits. That principle applies to anything that resembles something that you don't want your puppy to chew up.

COLLARS

A lightweight nylon collar is the best choice for a very young pup. Quick-clip collars are easy to put on and remove, and they can be adjusted as the puppy grows. Introduce him to his collar as soon as he comes home to get him accustomed to wearing it. He'll get used to it quickly and won't mind a bit. Make sure that it is snug enough that it won't slip off, yet loose enough to be comfortable for the pup. You should be able to slip two fingers between the collar and his neck. Check the collar often, as puppies grow in spurts, and his collar can become too tight almost overnight. Choke collars are for training purposes only and should never be used on a puppy under four or five months old.

LEASHES

A 6-foot nylon lead is an excellent choice for a young puppy. It is lightweight and not as tempting to chew as a leather lead. You can switch to a 6-foot leather lead after your pup has grown and is used to walking politely on a lead. For initial puppy walks and house-training purposes, you should invest in a

For everyday walks and explorations, a lightweight nylon leash will provide you with the comfort and control you need to train the pup.

Leash Life

Dogs love leashes! Believe it or not, most dogs dance for joy every time their owners pick up their leashes. The leash means that the dog is going for a walk—and there are few things more exciting than that! Here are some of the kinds of leashes that are commercially available.

Nylon Leash

Leather Leash

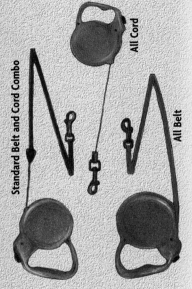

Standard Belt and Cord Combo

All Cord

All Belt

Retractable Leashes

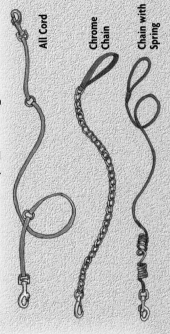

All Cord

Chrome Chain

Chain with Spring

Traditional Leash: Made of cotton, nylon or leather, these leashes are usually about 6 feet in length. A quality-made leather leash is softer on the hands than a nylon one. Durable woven cotton is a popular option. Lengths can vary up to about 48 feet, designed for different uses.

Chain Leash: Usually a metal chain leash with a plastic handle. This is not the best choice for most breeds, as it is heavier than other leashes and difficult to manage.

Retractable Leash: A long nylon cord is housed in a plastic device for extending and retracting. This leash is ideal for taking trained dogs for long walks in open areas, although it is not always suitable for large, powerful breeds. Different lengths and sizes are available, so check that you purchase one appropriate for your dog's weight.

Elastic Leash: A nylon leash with an elastic extension. This is useful for well-trained dogs, especially in conjunction with a head halter. Avoid leashes that are completely elastic, as they afford minimal control to the handler.

Adjustable Leash: This has two snaps, one on each end, and several metal rings. It is handy if you need to tether your dog temporarily, but is never to be used with a choke collar.

Tab Leash: A short leash (4 to 6 inches long) that attaches to your dog's collar. This device serves like a handle, in case you have to grab your dog while he's exercising off lead. It's ideal for "half-trained" dogs or dogs that listen only half of the time.

Slip Leash: Essentially a leash with a collar built in, similar to what a dog-show handler uses to show a dog. This British-style collar has a ring on the end so that you can form a slip collar. Useful if you have to catch your own runaway dog or a stray.

Adjustable Lead with Swivel

Loop with Sliding Bead

Martingale / Humane Choke

Show Lead with Sliding Clasp

Slip Noose

A Variety of Collar-and-Leash-in-One Products

shorter lead so that you have more control over the puppy. At first, you don't want him wandering too far away from you, and when taking him out for toileting you will want to keep him in the specific area chosen for his potty spot.

Once the puppy is heel trained with a traditional leash, you can consider purchasing a retractable lead. A retractable lead is excellent for walking adult dogs that are already leash-wise. This type of lead allows the dog to roam farther away

This tiny Fox Terrier pup has a long, bright future ahead of him. You are responsible for his everyday care and safety, from his grooming and sanitation needs to his protection and training.

from you and explore a wider area when out walking, and also retracts when you need to keep him close to you.

HOME SAFETY FOR YOUR PUPPY

The importance of puppy-proofing cannot be overstated. In addition to making your house comfortable for your Fox Terrier's arrival, you also must make sure that your house is safe for your puppy before you bring him home. There are countless hazards in the owner's personal living environment that a pup can sniff, chew, swallow or destroy. Many are obvious; others are not. Do a thorough advance house check to remove or rearrange those things that could hurt your puppy, keeping any potentially dangerous items out of areas to which he will have access.

FIRST CAR RIDE

The ride to your home from the breeder will no doubt be your puppy's first automobile experience, and you should make every effort to keep him comfortable and secure. Bring a large towel or small blanket for the puppy to lie on during the trip and an extra towel in case the pup gets carsick or has a potty accident. It's best to have another person with you to hold the puppy in his lap. Most puppies will fall fast asleep from the rolling motion of the car. If the ride is lengthy, you may have to stop so that the puppy can relieve himself, so be sure to bring a leash and collar for those stops. Avoid rest areas for potty trips, since those are frequented by many dogs, who may carry parasites or disease. It's better to stop at grassy areas near gas stations or shopping centers to prevent unhealthy exposure for your pup.

Fox Terriers, like most other dogs, love toys. Never offer them toys made for children, as they are neither strong enough nor non-toxic. Pet shops have huge selections of toys safe for dogs.

Electrical cords are especially dangerous, since puppies view them as irresistible chew toys. Unplug and remove all exposed cords or fasten them beneath a baseboard where the puppy cannot reach them. Veterinarians and firefighters can tell you horror stories about electrical burns and house fires that resulted from puppy-chewed electrical cords. Consider this a most serious precaution for your puppy and the rest of your family.

Scout your home for tiny objects that might be seen at a pup's eye level. Keep medication bottles and cleaning supplies well out of reach, and do the same with waste baskets and other trash containers. It goes without saying that you should not use rodent poison or other toxic chemicals in any puppy area and that you must keep such containers safely locked up. You will be amazed at how many places a curious puppy can discover.

Once your house has cleared inspection, check your yard. A sturdy fence, well embedded into the ground, will give your dog a safe place to play and potty. Although Fox Terriers are not known to be climbers or fence jumpers, they are still athletic dogs, so a 5- to 6-foot-high fence should be adequate to contain an agile youngster or adult. Check the fence periodically for necessary repairs. If there is a weak link or space to squeeze through, you can be sure a determined Fox Terrier will discover it.

The garage and shed can be hazardous places for a pup, as things like fertilizers, chemicals and tools are usually kept there. It's best to keep these areas off limits to the pup. Antifreeze is especially dangerous to dogs, as they find the taste appealing and it takes only a few licks from the driveway to kill a dog, puppy or adult, small breed or large.

VISITING THE VETERINARIAN

A good veterinarian is your Fox Terrier puppy's best health insurance policy. If you do not

SWEETS THAT KILL

Antifreeze would be every dog's favorite topping for a chocolate sundae! However, antifreeze, just like chocolate, kills dogs. Ethylene glycol, found in antifreeze, causes acute renal failure in dogs and can be fatal. Dogs suffering from kidney failure expel little or no urine, act lethargically, may experience vomiting or diarrhea and may resist activity and drinking water. Just a single teaspoon of antifreeze is enough to kill a dog (depending on the size); even for large dogs it takes only a tablespoon or two! Like that irresistible chocolate ice cream, antifreeze is sweet-tasting and smells yummy. Keep it away from your dog!.

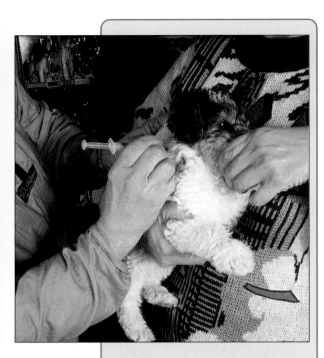

ASK THE VET

Help your vet help you to become a well-informed dog owner. Don't be shy about becoming involved in your puppy's veterinary care by asking questions and gaining as much knowledge as you can. For starters, ask what shots your puppy is getting and what diseases they prevent, and discuss with your vet the safest way to vaccinate. Find out what is involved in your dog's annual wellness visits. If you plan to spay or neuter, discuss the best age at which to have this done. Start out on the right "paw" with your puppy's vet and develop good communication with him, as he will care for your dog's health throughout the dog's entire life.

already have a vet, ask friends and experienced dog people in your area for recommendations so that you can select a vet before you bring your Fox Terrier puppy home. Also arrange for your puppy's first veterinary examination beforehand, since many vets have two- and three-week waiting periods and your puppy should visit the vet within a day or so of coming home.

It's important to make sure your puppy's first visit to the vet is a pleasant and positive one. The vet should take great care to befriend the pup and handle him gently to make their first meeting a positive experience. The vet will give the pup a thorough physical examination and set up a schedule for vaccinations and other necessary wellness visits. Be sure to show your vet any health and inoculation records, which you should have received from your breeder. Your vet is a great source of canine health information, so be sure to ask questions and take notes. Creating a health journal for your puppy will make a handy reference for his wellness and any future health problems that may arise.

MEETING THE FAMILY

Your Fox Terrier's homecoming is an exciting time for all members of the family, and it's only natural that everyone will be eager to meet him, pet him and play with him. However, for the puppy's sake, it's best to make these initial family meetings as uneventful as possible so that the pup is not overwhelmed with too much too soon. Remember, he has just left his dam and his littermates and is away from the breeder's home for the first time. Despite his fuzzy wagging tail, he is still apprehensive and wondering where he is and who all these strange humans are. It's best to let him explore on his own and meet the family members as he feels comfortable. Let him investigate all the new smells, sights and sounds at his own pace. Children should be especially careful to not get overly excited, use loud voices or hug the pup too tightly. Be calm, gentle and affectionate, and be ready to comfort him if he appears frightened or uneasy.

Be sure to show your puppy his new crate during this first day home. Toss a treat or two inside the crate; if he associates the crate with food, he will associate the crate with good things. If he is comfortable with the crate, you can offer him his first meal inside it. Leave the door ajar so he can wander in and out as he chooses.

FIRST NIGHT IN HIS NEW HOME

So much has happened in your Fox Terrier puppy's first day away from the breeder. He's had his first car ride to his new home. He's met his new human family

THE FAMILY TREE

Your puppy's pedigree is his family tree. Just as a child may resemble his parents and grandparents, so too will a puppy reflect the qualities, good and bad, of his ancestors, especially those in the first two generations. Therefore it's important to know as much as possible about a puppy's immediate relatives. Reputable and experienced breeders should be able to explain the pedigree and why they chose to breed from the particular dogs they used.

and perhaps the other family pets. He has explored his new house and yard, at least those places where he is to be allowed during his first weeks at home. He may have visited his new veterinarian. He has eaten his first meal or two away from his dam and litter-mates. Surely that's enough to tire out an eight-week-old Fox Terrier pup…or so you hope!

It's bedtime. During the day, the pup investigated his crate, which is his new den and sleeping space, so it is not entirely strange to him. Line the crate with a soft towel or blanket that he can snuggle into and gently place him into the crate for the night. Some breeders send home a piece of bedding from where the pup slept with his littermates, and those familiar scents are a great comfort

Mom taught her pup lots of life lessons, including how to speak "dog." It's the owner's responsibility to assume the pup's education, socialization and sensible care.

> ### BE CONSISTENT
> Consistency is a key element, in fact is absolutely necessary, to a puppy's learning environment. A behavior (such as chewing, jumping up or climbing onto the furniture) cannot be forbidden one day and then allowed the next. That will only confuse the pup, and he will not understand what he is supposed to do. Just one or two episodes of allowing an undesirable behavior to "slide" will imprint that behavior on a puppy's brain and make that behavior more difficult to erase or change.

for the puppy on his first night without his siblings.

He will probably whine or cry. The puppy is objecting to the confinement and the fact that he is alone for the first time. This can be a stressful time for you as well as for the pup. It's important that you remain strong and don't let the puppy out of his crate to comfort him. He will fall asleep eventually. If you release him, the puppy will learn that crying means "out" and will continue that habit. You are laying the groundwork for future habits. Some breeders find that soft music can soothe a crying pup and help him get to sleep.

SOCIALIZING YOUR PUPPY
The next 20 weeks of your Fox Terrier puppy's life are the most

important of his entire lifetime. A properly socialized puppy will grow up to be a confident and stable adult who will be a pleasure to live with and a welcome addition to the neighborhood.

The importance of socialization cannot be overemphasized. Research on canine behavior has proven that puppies who are not exposed to new sights, sounds, people and animals during their first 20 weeks of life will grow up to be timid and fearful, even aggressive, and unable to flourish outside of their home environment.

Socializing your puppy is not difficult and, in fact, will be a fun time for you both. Lead training goes hand in hand with socialization, so your puppy will be learning how to walk on a lead at the same time that he's meeting the neighborhood. Because the Fox Terrier is such a terrific breed, your puppy will enjoy being "the new kid on the block." Take him for short walks, to the park and to other dog-friendly places where he will encounter new people, especially children. Puppies automatically recognize children as "little people" and are drawn to play with them. Just make sure that you supervise these meetings and that the children do not get too rough or encourage him to play too hard. An overzealous pup can often nip too hard, frightening the child

and in turn making the puppy overly excited. A bad experience in puppyhood can impact a dog for life, so a pup that has a negative experience with a child may grow up to be shy or even aggressive around children.

Take your puppy along on your daily errands. Puppies are natural "people magnets," and most people who see your pup will want to pet him. All of these

Take nothing for granted. If your puppy has never had the chance to explore the great outdoors, it can be very overwhelming for him.

Also make sure that your puppy has received his first and second rounds of vaccinations before you expose him to other dogs or bring him to places that other dogs may frequent. Avoid dog parks and other strange-dog areas until your vet assures you that your puppy is fully immunized and resistant to the diseases that can be passed between canines. Discuss socialization with your breeder, as some breeders recommend socializing the puppy even before he has received all of his inoculations, depending on how outgoing the puppy may be.

LEADER OF THE PUPPY'S PACK
Like other canines, your puppy needs an authority figure, someone he can look up to and regard as the leader of his "pack." His first pack leader was his dam, who taught him to

Establish the house rules from day one. Do not allow the puppy on the sofa (even for photographs) if you do not intend to allow him access to your furniture. Be consistent, kind and fair when training the puppy.

encounters will help to mold him into a confident adult dog. Likewise, you will soon feel like a confident, responsible dog owner, rightly proud of your handsome Fox Terrier.

Be especially careful of your puppy's encounters and experiences during the eight-to-ten-week-old period, which is also called the "fear period." This is a serious imprinting period, and all contact during this time should be gentle and positive. A frightening or negative event could leave a permanent impression that could affect his future behavior if a similar situation arises.

THE FIRST FAMILY MEETING
Your puppy's first day at home should be quiet and uneventful. Despite his wagging tail, he is still wondering where his mom and siblings are! Let him make friends with other members of the family on his own terms; don't overwhelm him. You have a lifetime ahead to get to know each other!

be polite and not chew too hard on her ears or nip at her muzzle. He learned those same lessons from his littermates. If he played too rough, they cried in pain and stopped the game, which sent an important message to the rowdy puppy.

As puppies play together, they are also struggling to determine who will be the boss. Being pack animals, dogs need someone to be in charge. If a litter of puppies remained together beyond puppyhood, one of the pups would emerge as the strongest one, the one who calls the shots.

Once your puppy leaves the pack, he will look intuitively for a new leader. If he does not recognize you as that leader, he will try to assume that position for himself. Of course, it is hard to imagine your adorable Fox

Terrier puppy trying to be in charge when he is so small and seemingly helpless. You must remember that these are natural canine instincts. Do not cave in and allow your pup to get the upper "paw"!

Just as socialization is so important during these first 20

Puppies naturally accept humans as their caregivers and leaders. Are you ready to assume the lofty responsibility of taking care of a Fox Terrier puppy for his whole life?

MEET AND MINGLE

Puppies need to meet people and see the world if they are to grow up confident and unafraid. Take your puppy with you on everyday outings and errands. On-lead walks around the neighborhood and to the park offer the pup good exposure to the goings-on of his new human world. Avoid areas frequented by other dogs until your puppy has had his full round of puppy shots; ask your vet when your pup will be properly protected. Arrange for your puppy to meet new people of all ages every week.

weeks, so too is your puppy's early education. He was born without any bad habits. He does not know what is good or bad behavior. If he does things like nipping and digging, it's because he is having fun and doesn't know that humans consider these things as "bad." It's your job to teach him proper puppy manners, and this is the best time to accomplish that…before he has developed bad habits, since it is much more difficult to "unlearn" or correct unacceptable learned behavior than to teach good behavior from the start.

Make sure that all members of the family understand the importance of being consistent when training their new puppy. If you tell the puppy to stay off the

Fox Terriers remain "kids" for years! Be prepared for years of enjoyment and parenting with your Fox Terrier. This young Wire is ready for a game with his playmates.

TEETHING TIME

All puppies chew. It's normal canine behavior. Chewing just plain feels good to a puppy, especially during the three- to five-month teething period when the adult teeth are breaking through the gums. Rather than attempting to eliminate such a strong natural chewing instinct, you will be more successful if you redirect it and teach your puppy what he may or may not chew. Correct inappropriate chewing with a sharp "No!" and offer him a chew toy, praising him when he takes it. Don't become discouraged. Chewing usually decreases after the adult teeth have come in.

sofa and your daughter allows him to cuddle on the couch to watch her favorite television show, your pup will be confused about what he is and is not allowed to do. Have a family conference before your pup comes home so that everyone understands the basic principles of puppy training and the rules you have set forth for the pup, and agrees to follow them.

The old adage that "an ounce of prevention is worth a pound of cure" is especially true when it comes to puppies. It is much easier to prevent inappropriate behavior than it is to change it. It's also easier and less stressful for the pup, since it will keep discipline to a minimum and create a more positive learning environment for him. That, in turn, will also be easier on you!

Here are a few commonsense tips to keep your belongings safe and your puppy out of trouble:

- Keep your closet doors closed and your shoes, socks and other apparel off the floor so your puppy can't get at them.
- Keep a secure lid on the trash container or put the trash where your puppy can't dig into it. He can't damage what he can't reach!
- Supervise your puppy at all times to make sure he is not getting into mischief. If he starts to chew the corner of the rug, you can distract him instantly by tossing a toy for him to fetch. You also will be able to whisk him outside when you notice that he is about to piddle on the carpet. If you can't see your puppy, you can't teach or correct his behavior.

SOLVING PUPPY PROBLEMS

CHEWING AND NIPPING

Nipping at fingers and toes is normal puppy behavior. Chewing is also the way that puppies investigate their surroundings. However, you will have to teach your puppy that chewing anything other than his toys is not acceptable. That won't happen overnight and at times

puppy teeth will test your patience. However, if you allow nipping and chewing to continue, just think about the damage that a mature Fox Terrier can do with a full set of adult teeth.

Whenever your puppy nips your hand or fingers, cry out "Ouch!" in a loud voice, which should startle your puppy and stop him from nipping, even if only for a moment. Immediately distract him by offering a small treat or an appropriate toy for him to chew instead (which means having chew toys and puppy treats handy or in your pockets at all times). Praise him when he takes the toy and tell him what a good fellow he is. Praise is just as or even more important in puppy training as discipline and correction.

Puppies also tend to nip at children more often than adults, since they perceive little ones to be more vulnerable and more

Teething is a full-time occupation for puppies. Do not scold the puppy for chewing and massaging his teeth and gums. Give him safe chew toys and encourage him to use them whenever you see him chewing your clothing or furniture.

similar to their littermates. Teach your children appropriate responses to nipping behavior. If they are unable to handle it themselves, you may have to intervene. Puppy nips can be quite painful and a child's frightened reaction will only encourage a puppy to nip harder, which is a natural canine response. As with all other puppy situations, interaction between your Fox Terrier puppy and children should be supervised.

GOOD CHEWING

Chew toys run the gamut from rawhide chews to hard sterile bones and everything in between. Rawhides are all-time favorites, but they can cause choking when they become mushy from repeated chewing, causing them to break into small pieces that are easy to swallow. Rawhides are also highly indigestible, so many vets advise limiting rawhide treats. Hard sterile bones are great for plaque prevention as well as chewing satisfaction. Dispose of them when the ends become sharp or splintered.

Chewing on objects, not just family members' fingers and ankles, is also normal canine behavior that can be especially tedious (for the owner, not the pup) during the teething period when the puppy's adult teeth are coming in. At this stage, chewing just plain feels good. Furniture legs and cabinet corners are common puppy favorites. Shoes and other personal items also taste pretty good to a pup.

The best solution is, once again, prevention. If you value something, keep it tucked away and out of reach. You can't hide your dining-room table in a closet, but you can try to deflect the chewing by applying a bitter product made just to deter dogs from chewing. Available in a spray or cream, this substance is vile-tasting, although safe for dogs, and most puppies will avoid the forbidden object after one tiny taste. You also can apply the product to your leather leash if the puppy tries to chew on his lead during leash-training sessions.

Keep a ready supply of safe chews handy to offer your Fox Terrier as a distraction when he starts to chew on something that's a "no-no." Remember, at this tender age he does not yet know what is permitted or forbidden, so you have to be "on call" every minute he's awake and on the prowl.

You may lose a treasure or two during puppy's growing-up period, and the furniture could sustain a nasty nick or two. These can be trying times, so be prepared for those inevitable accidents and comfort yourself in knowing that this too shall pass.

JUMPING UP

Although Fox Terrier pups are not known to be notorious jumpers, they are still puppies after all, and puppies jump up...on you, your guests, your counters and your furniture. Just another normal part of growing up, and one you need to meet head-on before it becomes an ingrained habit.

The key to jump correction is consistency. You cannot correct your Fox Terrier for jumping up on you today, then allow it to happen tomorrow by greeting him with hugs and kisses. As you have learned by now, consistency is critical to all puppy lessons.

For starters, try turning your back as soon as the puppy jumps. Jumping up is a means of gaining your attention and, if the pup can't see your face, he may get discouraged and learn that he loses eye contact with his beloved master when he jumps up.

Leash corrections also work, and most puppies respond well to a leash tug if they jump. Grasp the leash close to the puppy's collar and give a quick tug

Fox Terriers have terrific balance and like to be up on their "toes." If jumping up is a problem with your dog, do not encourage him to practice his ballet steps.

downward, using the command "Off." Do not use the word "Down," since "Down" is used to teach the puppy to lie down, which is a separate action that he will learn during his education in the basic commands. As soon as the puppy has backed off, tell him to sit and immediately praise him for doing so. This will take many repetitions and won't be accomplished quickly, so don't

Your new puppy's first night in his new home may be unpleasant for all concerned. He'll be lonely and frightened and will be whining and crying to show his distress.

get discouraged or give up; you must be even more persistent than your puppy.

A second method used for jump correction is the spritzer bottle. Fill a spray bottle with water mixed with a bit of lemon juice or vinegar. As soon as puppy jumps, command him "Off" and spritz him with the water mixture. Of course, that means having the spray bottle handy whenever or wherever jumping usually happens.

Yet a third method to discourage jumping is grasping the puppy's paws and holding them gently but firmly until he struggles to get away. Wait a brief moment or two, then release his paws and give him a command to sit. He should eventually learn that jumping gets him into an uncomfortable predicament.

Children are major victims of puppy jumping, since puppies view little people as ready targets for jumping up as well as nipping. If your children (or their friends) are unable to dispense jump corrections, you will have to intervene and handle it for them.

Important to prevention is also knowing what you should not do. Never kick your Fox Terrier (for any reason, not just for jumping) or knock him in the chest with your knee. That maneuver could actually harm your puppy. Vets can tell you stories about puppies who suffered broken bones after being banged about when they jumped up.

PUPPY WHINING

Puppies often cry and whine, just as infants and little children do. It's their way of telling us that they are lonely or in need of attention. Your puppy will miss his littermates and will feel insecure when he is left alone. You may be out of the house or just in another room, but he will still feel alone. During these times, the puppy's crate should be his personal comfort station, a place all his own where he can feel safe and secure. Once he learns that being alone is okay and not something to be feared, he will settle down without crying or objecting. You might want to leave a radio on while he is crated, as the sound of human voices can be soothing and will give the impression that people are around.

Give your puppy a favorite cuddly toy or chew toy to entertain him whenever he is crated. You will both be happier: the puppy because he is safe in his den and you because he is quiet, safe and not getting into puppy escapades that can wreak havoc in your house or cause him danger.

To make sure that your puppy will always view his crate as a safe and cozy place, never, ever, use the crate as punishment. That's the best way to turn the crate into a negative place that the pup will want to avoid. Sure, you can use the crate for your own peace of mind if your puppy is getting into trouble and needs some "time out." Just don't let him know that! Never scold the pup

and immediately place him into the crate. Count to ten, give him a couple of hugs and maybe a treat, then scoot him into his crate.

It's also important not to make a big fuss when he is released from the crate. That will make getting out of the crate more appealing than being in the crate, which is just the opposite of what you are trying to achieve.

"COUNTER SURFING"
What we like to call "counter surfing" is a normal extension of jumping and usually starts to happen as soon as a puppy realizes that he is big enough to stand on his hind legs and investigate the good stuff on the kitchen counter or the coffee table. Once again, you have to be there to prevent it! As soon as you see your Fox Terrier even start to raise himself up, startle him with a sharp "No!" or "Aaahh, aaahh!" If he succeeds and manages to get one or both paws on the forbidden surface, smack those paws (firmly but gently) and tell him "Off!" As soon as he's back on all four paws, command him to sit and praise at once.

For surf prevention, make sure to keep any tempting treats or edibles out of reach, where your Fox Terrier can't see or smell them. It's the old rule of prevention yet again.

PROPER CARE OF YOUR

FOX TERRIER

Adding a Fox Terrier to your household means adding a new family member who will need your care each and every day. When your Fox Terrier pup first comes home, you will start a routine with him so that, as he grows up, your dog will have a daily schedule just as you do. The aspects of your dog's daily care will likewise become regular parts of your day, so you'll both have a new schedule. Dogs learn by consistency and thrive on routine: regular times for meals, exercise, grooming and potty trips are just as important for your dog as they are to you! Your dog's schedule will depend much on your family's daily routine, but remember that you now have a new member of the family who is part of your day every day.

> Healthy puppies look forward to mealtimes together and will happily compete for a place at the feeder. Once the puppy comes home, he may need a little encouragement to eat by himself. Within 24 hours, he should be comfortable dining alone.

FEEDING
Feeding your dog the best diet is based on various factors, including age, activity level, overall condition and size of breed. When you visit the breeder, he will share with you his advice about the proper diet for your dog based on his experience with the breed and the foods with which he has had success. Likewise, your vet will be a helpful source of advice throughout the dog's life and will aid you in planning a diet for optimal health.

FEEDING THE PUPPY
Of course, your pup's very first food will be his dam's milk. There may be special situations in which pups fail to nurse, necessitating that the breeder hand-feed them with a formula, but for the most part pups spend the first weeks of life nursing from their dam. The breeder weans the pups by gradually introducing solid foods and decreasing the milk meals. Pups may even start themselves off on the weaning process, albeit inadvertently, if

they snatch bites from their mom's food bowl.

By the time the pups are ready for new homes, they are fully weaned and eating a good puppy food. As a new owner, you may be thinking, "Great! The breeder has taken care of the hard part." Not so fast.

A puppy's first year of life is the time when all or most of his growth and development takes place. This is a delicate time, and diet plays a huge role in proper skeletal and muscular formation. Improper diet and exercise habits can lead to damaging problems that will compromise the dog's health and movement for his entire life. That being said, new owners should not worry needlessly. With the myriad types of food formulated specifically for growing pups of different-sized breeds, dog-food manufacturers have taken much of the guesswork out of feeding your puppy well. Since growth-food formulas are designed to provide the nutrition that a growing puppy needs, it is unnecessary and, in fact, can prove harmful to add supplements

to the diet. Research has shown that too much of certain vitamin supplements and minerals predispose a dog to skeletal problems. It's by no means a case of "if a little is good, a lot is better." At every stage of your dog's life, too

There is no food better for puppies under the age of six weeks than their mother's milk.

VARIETY IS THE SPICE
Although dog-food manufacturers contend that dogs don't like variety in their diets, studies show quite the opposite to be true. Dogs would much rather vary their meals than eat the same old chow day in and day out. Dry kibble is no more exciting for a dog than the same bowl of bran flakes would be for you. Fortunately, there are dozens of varieties available on the market, and your dog will likely show preference for certain flavors over others. A word of warning: don't overdo it or you'll develop a fussy eater who only prefers chopped beef fillet and asparagus tips every night.

The breeder likely fed the puppies three or four times a day. You will gradually cut meals back to two or three within the first few weeks.

growing puppies generally need proportionately more food per body weight than their adult counterparts, but a pup should never be allowed to gain excess weight. Dogs of all ages should be kept in proper body condition, but extra weight can strain a pup's developing frame, causing skeletal problems.

Watch your pup's weight as he grows and, if the recommended amounts seem to be too much or too little for your pup, consult the vet about appropriate dietary changes. Keep in mind that treats,

much or too little in the way of nutrients can be harmful, which is why a manufactured complete food is the easiest way to know that your dog is getting what he needs.

Because of a young pup's small body and accordingly small digestive system, his daily portion will be divided up into small meals throughout the day. This can mean starting off with three or more meals a day and decreasing the number of meals as the pup matures. Eventually you can feed only one meal a day, although it is generally thought that dividing the day's food into two meals on a morning/evening schedule is healthier for the dog's digestion.

Regarding the feeding schedule, feeding the pup at the same times and in the same place each day is important for both housebreaking purposes and establishing the dog's everyday routine. As for the amount to feed,

BARF THE WAY TO BETTER HEALTH

That's Biologically Appropriate Raw Food for your dog, as designed and trademarked by Dr. Ian Billinghurst. An alternative to feeding commercially prepared dog food from bags or cans that are known to contain numerous additives and preservatives, this diet aims to increase the longevity, overall health and reproductive abilities of dogs. The BARF diet is based on the feeding habits of wild or feral animals and thus includes whole raw animal- and plant-based foods as well as bones. In theory, BARF mimics the natural diets of dogs and contains muscle meat, bone, fat and organ meat plus vegetable matter. Many owners are very successful with the diet and others are not. Next time you visit your vet, ask him about BARF.

although small, can quickly add up throughout the day, contributing unnecessary calories. Treats are fine when used prudently; opt for dog treats specially formulated to be healthy or for nutritious snacks like small pieces of cheese or cooked chicken.

FEEDING THE ADULT DOG

For the adult (meaning physically mature) dog, feeding properly is about maintenance, not growth. Again, correct weight is a concern. Your dog should appear fit and should have an evident "waist." His ribs should not be protruding (a sign of being underweight), but they should be covered by only a slight layer of fat. Under normal circumstances, an adult dog can be maintained fairly easily with a high-quality nutritionally complete adult-formula food.

Factor treats into your dog's overall daily caloric intake, and avoid offering table scraps. Overweight dogs are more prone to health problems. Research has even shown that obesity takes years off a dog's life. With that in mind, resist the urge to overfeed and over-treat. Don't make unnecessary additions to your dog's diet, whether with tidbits or with extra vitamins and minerals.

The amount of food needed for proper maintenance will vary depending on the individual dog's activity level, but you will be able to tell whether the daily portions are keeping him in good shape. With the wide variety of good complete foods available, choosing what to feed is largely a matter of personal preference. Just as with the puppy, the adult dog should have consistency in his mealtimes and feeding place. In addition to a consistent routine, regular mealtimes also allow the owner to see how much his dog is eating. If the dog seems never to be satisfied or, likewise, becomes uninterested in his food, the owner will know right away that something is wrong and can consult the vet.

Feed your new puppy the same food to which he had become accustomed at the breeder's kennel. It can slowly be changed to another diet.

DIETS FOR THE AGING DOG

A good rule of thumb is that once a dog has reached 75% of his expected lifespan, he has reached "senior citizen" or geriatric status. Your Fox Terrier will be considered a senior at about 11–12 years of age; based on his size, he has a projected lifespan of about 14–16 years.

What does aging have to do with your dog's diet? No, he won't get a discount at the local diner's early-bird special. Yes, he will require some dietary changes to accommodate the changes that come along with increased age. One change is that the older dog's dietary needs become more similar to that of a puppy. Specifically, dogs can metabolize more protein as youngsters and seniors than in the adult-mainte-nance stage. Discuss with your vet whether you need to switch to a higher-protein or senior-formulated food or whether your current adult-dog food contains sufficient nutrition for the senior.

Watching the dog's weight remains essential, even more so in the senior stage. Older dogs are already more vulnerable to illness, and obesity only contributes to their susceptibility to problems. As the older dog becomes less active and thus exercises less, his regular portions may cause him to gain weight. At this point, you may consider decreasing his daily food intake or switching to a

DIET DON'TS

- Got milk? Don't give it to your dog! Dogs cannot tolerate large quantities of cows' milk, as they do not have the enzymes to digest lactose.
- You may have heard of dog owners who add raw eggs to their dogs' food for a shiny coat or to make the food more palatable, but consumption of raw eggs too often can cause a deficiency of the vitamin biotin.
- Avoid feeding table scraps, as they will upset the balance of the dog's complete food. Additionally, fatty or highly seasoned foods can cause upset canine stomachs.
- Do not offer raw meat to your dog. Raw meat can contain parasites; it also is high in fat.
- Vitamin A toxicity in dogs can be caused by too much raw liver, especially if the dog already gets enough vitamin A in his balanced diet, which should be the case.
- Bones like chicken, pork chop and other soft bones are not suitable, as they easily splinter.

reduced-calorie food. As with other changes, you should consult your vet for advice.

TYPES OF FOOD AND READING THE LABEL

When selecting the type of food to feed your dog, it is important to check out the label for ingredients. Many dry-food products have soybean, corn or rice as the main ingredient. The main ingredient will be listed first on the label, with the rest of the ingredients following in descending order according to their proportion in the food. While these types of dry food are fine, you should also look into dry foods based on meat or fish. These are better-quality foods and thus higher priced. However, they may be just as economical in the long run, because studies have shown that it takes less of the higher-quality foods to maintain a dog.

Comparing the various types of food, dry, canned and semi-moist, dry foods contain the least amount of water and canned foods the most. Proportionately, dry foods are the most calorie- and nutrient-dense, which means that you need more of a canned food product to supply the same amount of nutrition. In households domiciling breeds of disparate size, the canned/dry/semi-moist question can be of special importance. Larger breeds obviously eat more than smaller ones and thus in general do better on dry foods, but smaller breeds do fine on canned foods and require "small bite" formulations to protect their small mouths and teeth if fed only dry foods. So if you have breeds of different size in your household, consider both your own preferences and what your dogs like to eat, but in the main think canned for the little

guys and dry or semi-moist for everyone else. You may find success mixing the food types as well. Water is important for all dogs, but even more so for those fed dry foods, as there is no high water content in their food.

There are strict controls that regulate the nutritional content of dog food, and a food has to meet the minimum requirements in order to be considered "complete and balanced." It is important that you choose such a food for your dog, so check the label to be sure that your chosen food meets the requirements. If not, look for a food that clearly states on the label that it is formulated to be complete and balanced for your dog's particular stage of life.

Recommendations for amounts to feed will also be

Water should always be readily available to your Fox Terrier, especially when he's an adult. The water intake of puppies should be monitored closely to help make house-training more manageable.

Although Fox Terriers aren't commonly thought of as water dogs, they are terrific swimmers. Swimming is the best possible exercise for young dogs, as it does not stress the dog's growing joints and ligaments.

indicated on the label. You should also ask your vet about proper food portions, and you will keep an eye on your dog's condition to see whether the recommended amounts are adequate. If he becomes over- or underweight, you will need to make adjustments; this also would be a good time to consult your vet.

The food label may also make feeding suggestions, such as whether moistening a dry-food product is recommended. Sometimes a splash of water will make the food more palatable for the dog and even enhance the flavor. Don't be overwhelmed by the many factors that go into feeding your dog. Manufacturers

of complete and balanced foods make it easy, and once you find the right food and amounts for your Fox Terrier, his daily feeding will be a matter of routine.

DON'T FORGET THE WATER!

For a dog, it's always time for a drink! Regardless of what type of food he eats, there's no doubt that he needs plenty of water. Fresh cold water, in a clean bowl, should be freely available to your dog at all times. There are special circumstances, such as during puppy housebreaking, when you will want to monitor your pup's water intake so that you will be able to predict when he will need to relieve himself, but water must be available to him nonetheless. Water is essential for hydration and proper body function just as it is in humans.

You will get to know how much your dog typically drinks in a day. Of course, in the heat or if exercising vigorously, he will be more thirsty and will drink more. However, if he begins to drink noticeably more water for no apparent reason, this could signal any of various problems, and you are advised to consult your vet.

Water is the best drink for dogs. Some owners are tempted to give milk from time to time or to moisten dry food with milk, but dogs do not have the enzymes necessary to digest the lactose in milk, which is much different from the milk that nursing puppies receive. Therefore stick with clean fresh water to quench your dog's thirst, and always have it readily available to him.

EXERCISE
All terriers, whether the giant Airedale or the small Norfolk, require a good deal of exercise. The Fox Terrier is certainly no exception and he prefers to be active and busy. While a fair number of Fox Terriers can succumb to a lazy lifestyle, following their owners' example, most breed members need to run and release their pent-up terrier spirits. It is true that a sedentary

A game of fetch on land or water will be welcomed by your Fox Terrier. Be sure to exercise your dog in waters that are clean and free from pollutants or chemicals.

TWO'S COMPANY

One surefire method of increasing your adult dog's exercise plan is to adopt a second dog. If your dog is well socialized, he should take to his new canine pal in no time and soon the two will be giving each other lots of activity and exercise as they play, romp and explore together. Most owners agree that two dogs are hardly much more work than one. If you cannot afford a second dog, get together with a friend or neighbor who has a well-trained dog. Your dog will definitely enjoy the company of a new four-legged playmate.

lifestyle is as harmful to a dog as it is to a person, so never allow your Fox Terrier to become a "couch potato."

The Fox Terrier is a fairly active breed that enjoys exercise, but you don't have to be an Olympic athlete! Regular walks, play sessions in the backyard and letting the dog run free in a safely enclosed area under your

supervision are recommended forms of exercise for the Fox Terrier. For those who are more ambitious, you will find that your Fox Terrier also enjoys long walks, an occasional hike or even a swim! If your Fox Terrier is on the lazy side, bear in mind that an overweight dog should never be suddenly over-exercised; instead he should be allowed to increase exercise slowly. Not only is exercise essential to keep the dog's body fit, it is essential to his mental well-being. A bored dog will find something to do, which often manifests itself in some type of destructive behavior, such as digging and chewing. In this sense, keeping the Fox Terrier active and busy is essential for the owner's mental well-being as well.

GROOMING

Do understand when buying a dog that you have the responsibility of maintaining your dog. Think of it in terms of your child—you bathe your youngster, comb his hair and put clean clothes on him. The end product is that you have a child who smells good, looks tidy, and whom you enjoy having in your company. It is the same with your dog—keep the dog brushed, bathed and trimmed and you will find it a pleasure to be in his company. However, it will

Don't overdo the exercise of a puppy. You wouldn't expect your toddler to run a mile, so don't expect your puppy to keep up with your adult dog (or yourself).

require some effort to do this, and if you own a Wire rather than a Smooth, it will require quite a bit of effort.

The Wire is a double-coated dog. There is a dense, thick undercoat that protects the dog in all kinds of weather and there is a harsh outer coat. Coat care for the pet Wire can be very different and easier than the coat care for a show dog. The vast majority of Wire fanciers have dogs as pets and do not expect to maintain a show coat.

COAT CARE OF THE SMOOTH

For those with a Smooth Fox Terrier, grooming will consist of primarily a weekly once-over. Brush him with a bristle brush or glove. Take a damp face flannel and wipe down the entire body. Once a month or so, you may want to bathe him. You will find that this will loosen any dead coat, so after the bath be sure to brush him out thoroughly, as this will clean out any dead undercoat. After the dog is bathed it is also a good time to trim the toenails, as they will be soft and easier to trim. You may want to trim the whiskers to the skin; this will give the dog a neat, clean-cut look. Wipe him dry with a towel or use a hair dryer. If it is a nice sunny day, you may want to put him outside in his crate to dry. Never leave your dog crated in

direct sunlight for any length of time, as sunstroke is a common killer of dogs. If you are showing your Smooth, you may want to rub the dog down with a pomade or some other hair dressing to give his coat a high gloss. Trimming for show on a Smooth will be minimal and the purpose will be to neaten up the dog. *Voila!* You are finished! Smooth dogs are low maintenance and those of us who own one appreciate that fact.

Whether your new charge is a Smooth or a Wire, introduce him to grooming sessions from the very first day. He will enjoy the attention and get to look forward to your time together.

The only ways to achieve the proper show coat on a Wire is with a stripping knife or by hand-stripping.

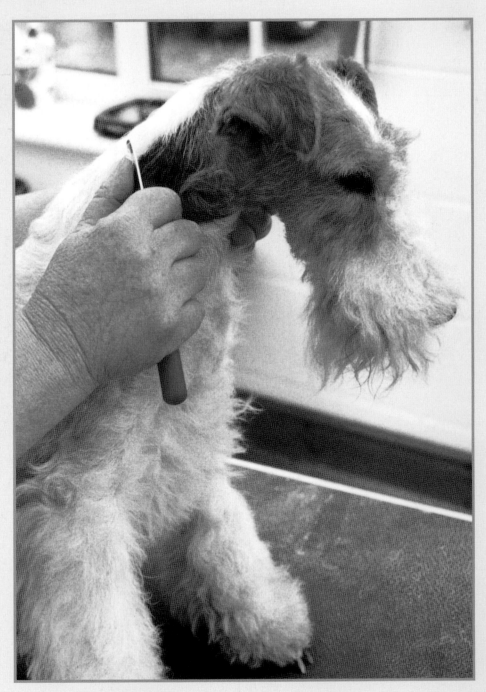

COAT CARE OF THE WIRE

If you are planning to show your Wire Fox Terrier, you will be ahead of the game if you purchase your puppy from a reputable breeder who grooms and shows his own dogs. If so, this is the individual to see for grooming lessons to learn how to get your dog ready for the show ring. Grooming for the show is an art, and an art that cannot be learned in a few months. Furthermore, it is very difficult, but not impossible, to learn it from a book, provided the budding groomer has some natural ability. The primary difference between the pet and show Wire coat is that the show dog will have a dense undercoat and on top of it he will have a shiny, harsh coat that will fit him like a jacket. With the proper coat, the dog presents a smartness in the ring that is hard to beat. This coat can only be acquired by stripping the body coat with a stripping knife or stripping by hand. Within eight to ten weeks, and with the proper upkeep, he will have grown from his "undergarment" stage into a smart new outfit ready for the ring. This all takes skill, time and talent in order to do it well.

Pet grooming is different from grooming for the show ring, as you use a clipper on the body and scissors for trimming the

furnishings. You will not have the harsh, tight-fitting jacket of the show Wire, but you will have a neat, clean and trimmed dog that will still look like a Wire Fox Terrier. Even those with kennels who are active in the show ring will clip their old dogs or those retired show dogs who are no longer being campaigned. A professional groomer is the best first approach to grooming a Wire Fox Terrier, even for a pet clip. Once you understand what is required to clipper the Wire, you may choose to undertake this

Start brushing your Fox Terrier as soon as you get him. This will accustom him to the grooming process and you won't have trouble when he grows up.

Selecting the Right Brushes and Combs

Will a rubber curry make my dog look slicker? Is a rake smaller than a pin brush? Do I choose nylon or natural bristles? Buying a dog brush can make the hairs on your head stand on end! Here's a quick once-over to educate you on the different types of brushes.

Slicker Brush: Fine metal prongs closely set on a curved base. Used to remove dead coat from the undercoat of medium- to long-coated breeds.

Pin Brush: Metal pins, often covered with rubber tips, set on an oval base. Used to remove shedding hair and is gentler than a slicker brush.

Metal Comb: Steel teeth attached to a steel handle; the closeness and size of the teeth vary greatly. A "flea comb" has tiny teeth set very closely together and is used to find fleas in a dog's coat. Combs with wider teeth are used for detangling longer coats.

Rake: Long-toothed comb with a short handle. Used to remove undercoat from heavily coated breeds with dense undercoats.

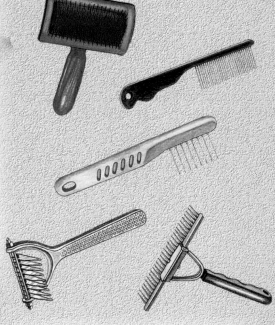

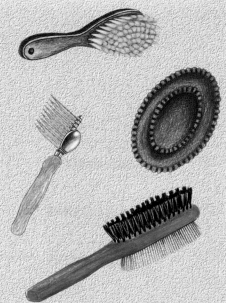

Soft-bristle Brush: Nylon or natural bristles set in a plastic or wood base. Used on short coats or long coats (without undercoats).

Rubber Curry: Rubber prongs, with or without a handle. Used for short-coated dogs. Good for use during shampooing.

Combination Brushes: Two-sided brush with a different type of bristle on each side; for example, pin brush on one side and slicker on the other, or bristle brush on one side and pin brush on the other. An economical choice if you need two kinds of brushes.

Grooming Glove: Sometimes called a hound glove; used to give sleek-coated dogs a once-over.

procedure on your own.

Here are the tools that you will need if you are going to do your own grooming:

1. A grooming table, something sturdy with a rubber mat covering the top. You will need a grooming arm, or a "hanger." (You can use a small sturdy table with an eye hook in the ceiling for holding the leash.) Your dog will now be comfortable even if confined and you will be able to work on the dog. Grooming is a very difficult and frustrating job if you try to groom without a table and a grooming arm.
2. A metal comb.
3. A slicker brush.
4. A good sharp pair of scissors.
5. A toenail trimmer.
6. Electric clippers with a #10 blade.

To start, set your dog on the table and put the leash around his neck. Have your leash up behind the ears and have the leash taut when you fasten it to your eye hook. Do not walk away and leave your dog unattended, as he can jump off the table and be left dangling from the leash with his feet scrambling around in the air.

Take your slicker brush and brush out the entire coat. Brush the whiskers toward the nose, the body hair toward the tail, the tail up toward the tip of the tail. Brush the leg furnishings up toward the body and brush the chest hair down toward the table. Hold the dog up by the front legs and gently brush the stomach hair, first toward the head and then back toward the rear. For cleanliness, you may want to take your scissors and trim the area around the penis. With the girls, trim some of the hair around the vulva.

Now that your dog is brushed out, comb through the coat with your metal comb. By now you have removed a fair amount of dead hair and your dog will already be looking better. You may find some small mats and these can be worked out with your fingers or your comb. If you brush your dog out every week or so, you will not have too much of a problem with mats.

We are now at the stage where you will take your clippers in hand. This, of course, is the most difficult part of grooming the pet Wire. Fortunately, your dog will only need to be clipped every three

Rely on the advice and instruction of an experienced handler or groomer to show you how to groom the Wire Fox's coat. He should be kept tidy and his coat hard and wiry, like his namesake.

Using a proper grooming table makes the task much easier.

months or so, but you may want to touch up the head more often.

Be sure to trim in the direction that the hair lies. Now take your comb and comb the leg hair down toward the table. Take your scissors and trim the legs neatly. The front legs should look like cylinders and the beard should have a squared-off look.

Take your scissors and trim off anything that sticks out. If this is your first time grooming the pet Wire on your own, you may be a bit clumsy, so be very careful not to harm the dog or damage the coat. The finished product may not be quite what you had expected, but practice and experience will pay off and you will soon be very proud of your efforts.

Put your dog in the bath when you are finished and give him a good washing and rinsing. After toweling him, return him to the grooming table and trim the toenails on all four legs. At this point you can dry your dog with a blow dryer and brush him out again. Or you can let him dry naturally and then brush him out.

Your pet should be brushed weekly and bathed as needed. Trim the toenails every month or so and plan to clip the dog every three months. Follow this plan and your dog will be clean, he will have a new outfit every three months, and he will look like a Wire Fox Terrier!

BATHING
In general, dogs need to be bathed only a few times a year, possibly

more often if your dog gets into something messy or if he starts to smell like a dog. Show dogs are usually bathed before every show, which could be as frequent as weekly, although this depends on the owner. Bathing too frequently can have negative effects on the skin and coat, removing natural oils and causing dryness.

If you give your dog his first bath when he is young, he will become accustomed to the process. Wrestling a dog into the tub or chasing a freshly shampooed dog who has escaped from the bath will be no fun! Most dogs don't naturally enjoy their baths, but you at least want yours to cooperate with you.

Before bathing the dog, have the items you'll need close at hand. First, decide where you will bathe the dog. You should have a tub or basin with a non-slip surface. Puppies can even be bathed in a sink. In warm weather, some like to use a portable pool in the yard, although you'll want to make sure your dog doesn't head for the nearest dirt pile following his bath! You will also need a hose or shower spray to wet the coat thoroughly, a shampoo formulated for dogs, absorbent towels and

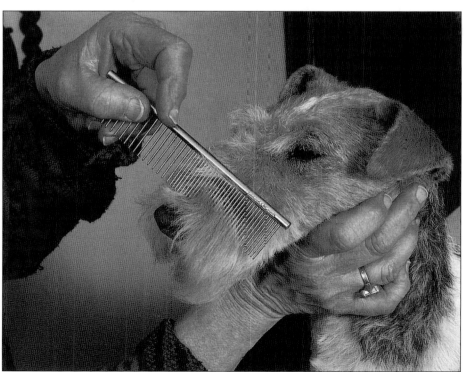

Hold the dog's head firmly as you use the comb around his face. The Wire should have a properly coifed beard.

perhaps a blow dryer. Human shampoos are too harsh for dogs' coats and will dry them out.

Before wetting the dog, give him a brush-through to remove any dead hair, dirt and mats. Make sure he is at ease in the tub and have the water at a comfortable temperature. Begin bathing by wetting the coat all the way down to the skin. Massage in the shampoo, keeping it away from his face and eyes. Rinse him thoroughly, again avoiding the eyes and ears, as you don't want to get water into the ear canals. A thorough rinsing is important, as shampoo residue is drying and itchy to the dog. After rinsing, wrap him in a towel to absorb the initial moisture. You can finish drying with either a towel or a blow dryer on low heat, held at a

Your vet can recommend a quality ear-cleaning solution for your Fox Terrier.

THE EARS KNOW

Examining your puppy's ears helps ensure good internal health. The ears are the eyes to the dog's innards! Begin handling your puppy's ears when he's still young so that he doesn't protest every time you lift a flap or touch his ears. Yeast and bacteria are two of the culprits that you can detect by examining the ear. You will notice a strong, often foul, odor, debris, redness or some kind of discharge. All of these point to health problems that can worsen over time. Additionally, you are on the lookout for wax accumulation, ear mites and other tiny bothersome parasites and their even tinier droppings. You may have to pluck hair with tweezers in order to have a better view into the dog's ears, but this is painless if done carefully.

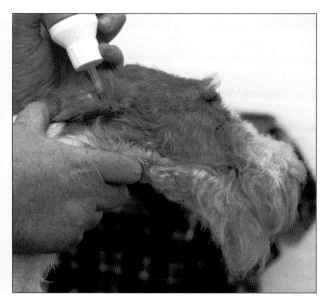

safe distance from the dog. You should keep the dog indoors and away from drafts until he is completely dry.

NAIL CLIPPING

Having his nails trimmed is not on many dogs' lists of favorite things to do. With this in mind, you will need to accustom your puppy to the procedure at a young age so that he will sit still (well, as still as he can) for his pedicures. Long nails can cause the dog's feet to spread, which is not good for him; likewise, long nails can hurt if they unintentionally scratch, not good for you!

Some dogs' nails are worn down naturally by regular walking on hard surfaces, so the frequency with which you clip depends on your individual dog. Look at his nails from time to time and clip as needed; a good way to know when it's time for a trim is if you hear your dog clicking as he walks across the floor.

There are several types of nail clippers and even electric nail-grinding tools made for dogs. First we'll discuss using the clipper. To start, have your clipper ready and

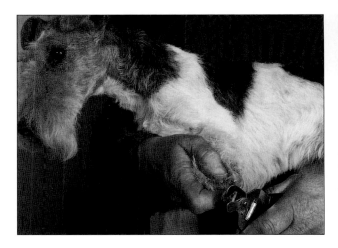

some doggie treats on hand. You want your pup to view his nail-clipping sessions in a positive light, and what better way to convince him than with food? You may want to enlist the help of an assistant to comfort the pup and offer treats as you concentrate on the clipping itself. The guillotine-type clipper is thought of by many as the easiest type to use; the nail tip is inserted into the opening, and blades on the top and bottom snip it off in one clip.

Start by grasping the pup's paw; a little pressure on the foot pad causes the nail to extend, making it easier to clip. Clip off a little at a time. If you can see the "quick," which is a blood vessel that runs through each nail, you will know how much to trim, as you do not want to cut into the quick. On that note, if you do cut the quick, which will cause bleeding, you can stem the flow of

Trim your dog's toenails after the bath; they will be softer then.

The guillotine-style nail clippers are the easiest to use, especially on a puppy. Actually they are so user-friendly that a child can handle them—but under proper supervision, of course.

Never drive with dogs loose within the vehicle. Use a crate or harness whenever transporting your dog.

blood with a styptic pencil or other clotting agent. If you mistakenly nip the quick, do not panic or fuss, as this will cause the pup to be afraid. Simply reassure the pup, stop the bleeding and move on to the next nail. Don't be discouraged; you will become a professional canine pedicurist with practice.

You may or may not be able to see the quick, so it's best to just clip off a small bit at a time. If you see a dark dot in the center of the nail, this is the quick and your cue to stop clipping. Tell the puppy he's a "good boy" and offer a piece of treat with each nail. You can also use nail-clipping time to examine the footpads, making sure that they are not dry and cracked and that nothing has become embedded in them.

The nail grinder, the second choice, is many owners' first choice. Accustoming the puppy to the sound of the grinder and sensation of the buzz presents fewer challenges than the clipper, and there's no chance of cutting through the quick. Use the grinder on a low setting and always talk soothingly to your dog. He won't mind his salon visit, and he'll have nicely polished nails as well.

HIT THE ROAD

Car travel with your Fox Terrier may be limited to necessity only, such as trips to the vet, or you

may bring your dog along almost everywhere you go. This will depend much on your individual dog and how he reacts to rides in the car. You can begin desensitizing your dog to car travel as a pup so that it's something that he's used to. Still, some dogs suffer from motion sickness. Your vet may prescribe a medication for this if trips in the car pose a problem for your dog. At the very least, you will need to get him to the vet, so he will need to tolerate these trips with the least amount of hassle possible.

Start taking your pup on short trips, maybe just around the block to start. If he is fine with short trips, lengthen your rides a little at a time. Start to take him on your errands or just for drives around town. By this time it will be easy to tell whether your dog is a born traveler or would prefer staying at home when you are on the road.

Of course, safety is a concern for dogs in the car. First, he must travel securely, not left loose to roam about the car where he could be injured or distract the driver. A young pup can be held by a passenger initially but should soon graduate to a travel crate, which can be the same crate he uses in the home. Other options include a car harness (like a seat belt for dogs) and partitioning the back of the car with a gate made for this purpose.

Bring along what you will need for the dog. He should wear his collar and ID tags, of course, and you should bring his leash, water (and food if a long trip) and clean-up materials for potty breaks and in case of motion sickness. Always keep your dog on his leash when you make stops, and never leave him alone in the car. Many a dog has died from the heat inside a closed car; this does not take much time at all. A dog left alone inside a car can also be a target for thieves.

ID FOR YOUR DOG

You love your Fox Terrier and want to keep him safe. Of course you take every precaution to prevent his escaping from the yard or becoming lost or stolen. You have a sturdy high fence and you always keep your dog on lead when out and about in public places. If your dog is not properly identified, however, you are overlooking a major aspect of his safety. We hope to never be in a situation where our dog is missing, but we should practice prevention in the unfortunate case that this happens; identification greatly increases the chances of your dog's being returned to you

There are several ways to identify your dog. First, the traditional dog tag should be a staple in your dog's wardrobe, attached to his everyday collar. Tags can be made of sturdy

You will need to apply for a dog license, though it does not include driving privileges. No matter how bright and talented your Fox Terrier is, he must travel in his crate where he will be safe and not have to worry about traffic laws.

Road trip! This fast-growing clan of Wire Foxes is ready for anything. Most dogs enjoy traveling by car, though owners must keep safety foremost in their minds.

plastic and various metals and should include your contact information so that a person who finds the dog can get in touch with you right away to arrange his return. Many people today enjoy the wide range of decorative tags available, so have fun and create a tag to match your dog's personality. Of course, it is important that the tag stays on the collar, so have a secure "O" ring attachment; you also can explore the type of tag that slides right onto the collar.

In addition to the ID tag, which every dog should wear even if identified by another method, two other forms of identification have become popular: microchipping and tattooing. In microchipping, a tiny scannable chip is painlessly inserted under the dog's skin. The number is registered to you so that, if your lost dog turns up at a clinic or shelter, the chip can be scanned to retrieve your contact information.

The advantage of the microchip is that it is a permanent form of ID, but there are some factors to consider. Several different companies make microchips, and not all are compatible with the others' scanning devices. It's best to find a company with a universal microchip that can be read by scanners made by other companies as well. It won't do any good to have the dog chipped if the information cannot be retrieved. Also, not every humane society, shelter and clinic is equipped with a scanner, although more and more facilities are equipping themselves. In fact, many shelters microchip dogs that they adopt out to new homes.

In the US, there are five or six major microchip manufacturers as well as a few databases. The American Kennel Club's Companion Animal Recovery unit works in conjunction with HomeAgain™ Companion Animal Retrieval System (Schering-Plough). In the UK, The Kennel

Club is affiliated with the National Pet Register, operated by Wood Green Animal Shelters.

Because the microchip is not visible to the eye, the dog must wear a tag that states that he is microchipped so that whoever picks him up will know to have him scanned. He of course also should have a tag with contact information in case his chip cannot be read. Humane societies and veterinary clinics offer this service, which is usually very affordable.

Though less popular than microchipping, tattooing is another permanent method of ID for dogs. Most vets perform this service, and there are also clinics that perform dog tattooing. This is also an affordable procedure and one that will not cause much discomfort for the dog. It is best to put the tattoo in a visible area, such as the ear, to deter theft. It is sad to say that there are cases of dogs' being stolen and sold to research laboratories, but such laboratories will not accept tattooed dogs.

To ensure that the tattoo is effective in aiding your dog's return to you, the tattoo number must be registered with a national organization. That way, when someone finds a tattooed dog a phone call to the registry will quickly match the dog with his owner.

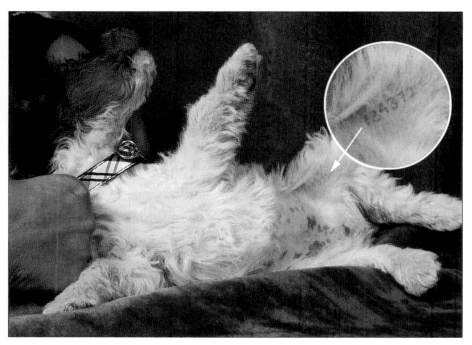

Your local veterinarian should be able to tattoo your puppy to protect him from dognapping and to enable others to return him should he become lost.

FOX TERRIER

BASIC TRAINING PRINCIPLES: PUPPY VS. ADULT

There's a big difference between training an adult dog and training a young puppy. With a young puppy, everything is new. At eight to ten weeks of age, he will be experiencing many things, and he has nothing with which to compare these experiences. Up to this point, he has been with his dam and littermates, not one-on-one with people except in his interactions with his breeder and visitors to the litter.

When you first bring the puppy home, he is eager to please you. This means that he accepts doing things your way. During the next couple of months, he will absorb the basis of everything he needs to know for the rest of his life. This early age is even referred to as the "sponge" stage. After that, for the next 18 months, it's up to you to reinforce good manners by building on the foundation that you've established. Once your puppy is reliable in basic commands and behavior and has reached the appropriate age, you may gradually introduce him to some of the interesting sports, games and activities available to pet owners and their dogs.

Raising your puppy is a family affair. Each member of the family must know what rules to set forth for the puppy and how to use the same one-word commands to mean exactly the same thing every time. Even if yours is a large family, one person will soon be considered by the pup to be the leader, the Alpha person in his pack, the "boss" who must be obeyed. Often that highly regarded person turns out to be the one who feeds the puppy.

OUR CANINE KIDS

"Everything I learned about parenting, I learned from my dog." How often adults recognize that their parenting skills are mere extensions of the education they acquired while caring for their dogs. Many owners refer to their dogs as their "kids" and treat their canine companions like real members of the family. Surveys indicate that a majority of dog owners talk to their dogs regularly, celebrate their dogs' birthdays and purchase Christmas gifts for their dogs. Another survey shows that dog owners take their dogs to the veterinarian more frequently than they visit their own physicians.

Food ranks very high on the puppy's list of important things! That's why your puppy is rewarded with small treats along with verbal praise when he responds to you correctly. As the puppy learns to do what you want him to do, the food rewards are gradually eliminated and only the praise remains. If you were to keep up with the food treats, you could have two problems on your hands—an obese dog and a beggar.

Training begins the minute your Fox Terrier puppy steps through the doorway of your home, so don't make the mistake of putting the puppy on the floor and telling him by your actions to "Go for it! Run wild!" Even if this is your first puppy, you must act as if you know what you're doing: be the boss. An uncertain pup may be terrified to move, while a bold one will be ready to take you at your word and start plotting to destroy the house! Before you collected your puppy, you decided where his own special place would be, and that's where to put him when you first arrive home. Give him a house tour after he has investigated his area and had a nap and a bathroom "pit stop."

It's worth mentioning here that, if you've adopted an adult dog that is completely trained to your liking, lucky you! You're off the hook! However, if that dog

spent his life up to this point in a kennel, or even in a good home but without any real training, be prepared to tackle the job ahead. A dog three years of age or older with no previous training cannot be blamed for not knowing what he was never taught. While the dog is trying to understand and learn your rules, at the same time he has to unlearn many of his previously self-taught habits and

Schooldays begin on day one. Imprinting your scent on the puppy, making him feel secure and earning his trust are the groundwork for a dog's education.

THE RIGHT START

The best advice for a potential dog owner is to start with the very best puppy that money can buy. Don't shop around for a bargain in the newspaper. You're buying a companion, not a used Buick or a second-hand Maytag. The purchase price of the dog represents a very significant part of the investment, but this is indeed a very small sum compared to the expenses of maintaining the dog in good health. If you purchase a well-bred healthy and sound puppy, you will be starting right. An unhealthy puppy can cost you thousands of dollars in unnecessary veterinary expenses and, possibly, a fortune in heartbreak as well.

general view of the world.

Working with a professional trainer will speed up your progress with an adopted adult dog. You'll need patience, too. Some new rules may be close to impossible for the dog to accept. After all, he's been successful so far by doing everything his way! (Patience again.) He may agree with your instruction for a few days and then slip back into his old ways, so you must be just as consistent and understanding in your teaching as you would be with a puppy. (More patience needed yet again!) Your dog has to learn to pay attention to your voice, your family, the daily routine, new smells, new sounds and, in some cases, even a new climate.

One of the most important things to find out about a newly adopted adult dog is his reaction to children (yours and others), strangers and your friends, and how he acts upon meeting other dogs. If he was not socialized with dogs as a puppy, this could be a major problem. This does not mean that he's a "bad" dog, a vicious dog or an aggressive dog; rather, it means that he has no idea how to read another dog's body language. There's no way for him to tell whether the other dog is a friend or foe. Survival instinct takes over, telling him to attack first and ask questions later. This definitely calls for professional help and, even then, may not be a behavior that can be corrected 100% reliably (or even at all). If you have a puppy, this is why it is so very important to introduce your young puppy properly to other puppies and "dog-friendly" adult dogs.

HOUSE-TRAINING YOUR FOX TERRIER

Dogs are tactility-oriented when it comes to house-training. In other words, they respond to the surface on which they are given approval to eliminate. The choice is yours (the dog's version is in parentheses): The lawn (including the neighbors' lawns)? A bare patch of earth under a tree (where people like to sit and relax in the

WHO'S TRAINING WHOM?

Dog training is a black-and-white exercise. The correct response to a command must be absolute, and the trainer must insist on completely accurate responses from the dog. A trainer cannot command his dog to sit and then settle for the dog's melting into the down position. Often owners are so pleased that their dogs "did something" in response to a command that they just shrug and say, "OK, Down" even though they wanted the dog to sit. You want your dog to respond to the command without hesitation: he must respond at that moment and correctly every time.

summertime)? Concrete steps or patio (all sidewalks, garage and basement floors)? The curbside (watch out for cars)? A small area of crushed stone in a corner of the yard (mine!)? The latter is the best choice if you can manage it, because it will remain strictly for the dog's use and is easy to keep clean.

You can start out with paper-training indoors and switch over to an outdoor surface as the puppy matures and gains control over his need to eliminate. For the nay-sayers, don't worry—this won't mean that the dog will soil on every piece of newspaper lying around the house. You are

When trained from an early age, a Fox Terrier will obey all members of the family with whom the dog has established a bond of trust.

Grass is the natural choice for a Fox Terrier's relief site. It smells and feels the best. Encourage your puppy to use the same area every time he's "got to go."

first thing in the morning until his bedtime! That's a total of ten or more trips per day to teach the puppy where it's okay to relieve himself. With that schedule in mind, you can see that house-training a young puppy is not a part-time job. It requires someone to be home all day.

If that seems overwhelming or impossible, do a little planning. For example, plan to pick up your puppy at the start of a vacation period. If you can't get home in the middle of the day, plan to hire a dog-sitter or ask a neighbor to come over to take the pup outside, feed him his lunch and then take him out again about ten or so

training him to go outside, remember? Starting out by paper-training often is the only choice for a city dog.

WHEN YOUR PUPPY'S "GOT TO GO"
Your puppy's need to relieve himself is seemingly non-stop, but signs of improvement will be seen each week. From 8 to 10 weeks old, the puppy will have to be taken outside every time he wakes up, about 10-15 minutes after every meal and after every period of play—all day long, from

POTTY COMMAND
Most dogs love to please their masters; there are no bounds to what dogs will do to make their owners happy. The potty command is a good example of this theory. If toileting on command makes the master happy, then more power to him. Puppies will obligingly piddle if it really makes their keepers smile. Some owners can be creative about which word they will use to command their dogs to relieve themselves. Some popular choices are "Potty," "Tinkle," "Piddle," "Let's go," "Hurry up" and "Toilet." Give the command every time your puppy goes into position and the puppy will begin to associate his business with the command.

blender and dishwasher. He will also be enchanted by the smell of your cooking (and will never be critical when you burn something). An exercise pen (also called an "ex-pen," a puppy version of a playpen) within the room of choice is an excellent means of confinement for a young pup. He can see out and has a certain amount of space in which to run about, but he is safe from dangerous things like electrical cords, heating units, trash baskets

Every puppy is unique and learns at his own pace. Be patient with your puppy and your consistency and kindness will pay off in no time.

minutes after he's eaten. Also make arrangements with that or another person to be your "emergency" contact if you have to stay late on the job. Remind yourself—repeatedly—that this hectic schedule improves as the puppy gets older.

HOME WITHIN A HOME

Your Fox Terrier puppy needs to be confined to one secure, puppy-proof area when no one is able to watch his every move. Generally the kitchen is the place of choice because the floor is washable. Likewise, it's a busy family area that will accustom the pup to a variety of noises, everything from pots and pans to the telephone,

or open kitchen-supply cabinets. Place the pen where the puppy will not get a blast of heat or air conditioning.

In the pen, you can put a few toys, his bed (which can be his crate if the dimensions of pen and crate are compatible) and a few layers of newspaper in one small corner, just in case. A water bowl can be hung at a convenient height on the side of the ex-pen so it won't become a splashing pool for an innovative puppy. His food dish can go on the floor, near but not under the water bowl.

Crates are something that pet owners are at last getting used to for their dogs. Wild or domestic canines have always preferred to sleep in den-like safe spots, and that is exactly what the crate provides. How often have you seen adult dogs that choose to sleep under a table or chair even though they have full run of the house? It's the den connection.

In your "happy" voice, use

If you choose to buy a bed for your puppy, make sure it's durable and washable. Wait until he's completely housebroken to buy him the four-poster bed in the doggie catalog!

the word "Crate" every time you put the pup into his den. If he's new to a crate, toss in a small biscuit for him to chase the first few times. At night, after he's been outside, he should sleep in his crate. The crate may be kept in his designated area at night or, if you want to be sure to hear those wake-up yips in the morning, put the crate in a corner of your bedroom. However, don't make any response whatsoever to whining or crying. If he's completely ignored, he'll settle down and get to sleep.

Good bedding for a young puppy is an old folded bath towel or an old blanket, something that is easily washable and disposable if necessary ("accidents" will happen!). Never put newspaper in the puppy's crate. Also those old ideas about adding a clock to replace his mother's heartbeat, or a hot-water bottle to replace her warmth, are just that—old ideas. The clock could drive the puppy nuts, and the hot-water bottle could end up as a very soggy waterbed! An extremely good breeder would have introduced your puppy to the crate by letting two pups sleep together for a couple of nights, followed by several nights alone. How thankful you will be if you found that breeder!

Safe toys in the pup's crate or area will keep him occupied, but monitor their condition closely.

Discard any toys that show signs of being chewed to bits. Squeaky parts, bits of stuffing or plastic or any other small pieces can cause intestinal blockage or possibly choking if swallowed.

PROGRESSING WITH POTTY-TRAINING
After you've taken your puppy out and he has relieved himself in the area you've selected, he can have some free time with the family as long as there is someone responsible for watching him. That doesn't mean just someone in the same room who is watching TV or busy on the computer, but one person who is doing nothing other than keeping an eye on the pup, playing with him on the floor and helping him understand his position in the pack.

This first taste of freedom will let you begin to set the house

Your puppy's nose is a mighty organ—don't underestimate it. Watch him follow it and how he responds to the information he receives from it. You're training that nose along with his brain and private parts.

rules. If you don't want the dog on the furniture, now is the time to prevent his first attempts to jump up onto the couch. The word to use in this case is "Off," not "Down." "Down" is the word you will use to teach the down position, which is something entirely different.

Most corrections at this stage come in the form of simply distracting the puppy. Instead of telling him "No" for "Don't chew the carpet," distract the chomping puppy with a toy and he'll forget about the carpet.

As you are playing with the pup, do not forget to watch him closely and pay attention to his body language. Whenever you see him begin to circle or sniff, take the puppy outside to relieve himself. If you are paper-training, put him back into his confined area on the newspapers. In either case, praise him as he eliminates while he actually is in the act of relieving himself. Three seconds

CREATURES OF HABIT

Canine behaviorists and trainers aptly describe dogs as "creatures of habit," meaning that dogs respond to structure in their daily lives and welcome a routine. Do not interpret this to mean that dogs enjoy endless repetition in their training sessions. Dogs get bored just as humans do. Keep training sessions interesting and exciting. Vary the commands and the locations in which you practice. Give short breaks for play in between lessons. A bored student will never be the best performer in the class.

EXTRA! EXTRA!

The headlines read: "Puppy Piddles Here!" Breeders commonly use newspapers to line their whelping pens, so puppies learn to associate newspapers with relieving themselves. Do not use newspapers to line your pup's crate, as this will signal to your puppy that it is OK to urinate in his crate. If you choose to paper-train your puppy, you will layer newspapers on a section of the floor near the door he uses to go outside. You should encourage the puppy to use the papers to relieve himself, and bring him there whenever you see him getting ready to go. Little by little, you will reduce the size of the newspaper-covered area so that the puppy will learn to relieve himself "on the other side of the door."

after he has finished is too late! You'll be praising him for running toward you, or picking up a toy or whatever he may be doing at that moment, and that's not what you want to be praising him for. Timing is a vital tool in all dog training. Use it.

Remove soiled newspapers immediately and replace them with clean ones. You may want to take a small piece of soiled paper and place it in the middle of the new clean papers, as the scent will attract him to that spot when it's time to go again. That scent attraction is why it's so important

to clean up any messes made in the house by using a product specially made to eliminate the odor of dog urine and droppings. Regular household cleansers won't do the trick. Pet shops sell the best pet deodorizers. Invest in the largest container you can find.

Scent attraction eventually will lead your pup to his chosen spot outdoors; this is the basis of outdoor training. When you take your puppy outside to relieve himself, use a one-word command such as "Outside" or "Go-potty" (that's one word to the puppy!) as you pick him up and attach his leash. Then put him down in his area. If for any reason you can't carry him, snap the leash on quickly and lead him to his spot. Now comes the hard part—hard for you, that is. Just stand there until he urinates and defecates. Move him a few feet in one direction or another if he's just sitting there looking at you, but remember that this is neither playtime nor time for a walk. This is strictly a business trip! Then, as he circles and squats (remember your timing!), give him a quiet "Good dog" as praise. If you start to jump for joy, ecstatic over his performance, he'll do one of two things: either he will stop mid-stream, as it were, or he'll do it again for you—in the house—and expect you to be just as delighted!

Give him five minutes or so and, if he doesn't go in that time, take him back indoors to his confined area and try again in another ten minutes, or immediately if you see him sniffing and circling. By careful observation, you'll soon work out a successful schedule.

Accidents, by the way, are just that—accidents. Clean them up quickly and thoroughly, without comment, after the puppy has been taken outside to finish his business and then put back into his area or crate. If you witness an accident in progress, say "No!" in a stern voice and get the pup outdoors immediately. No punishment is needed. You and your puppy are just learning each other's language, and sometimes it's easy to miss a puppy's message. Chalk it up to experience and watch more closely from now on.

KEEPING THE PACK ORDERLY

Discipline is a form of training that brings order to life. For example, military discipline is what allows the soldiers in an army to work as one. Discipline is a form of teaching and, in dogs, is the basis of how the successful pack operates. Each member knows his place in the pack and all respect the leader, or Alpha dog. It is essential for your puppy that you establish this type of relationship, with you as the Alpha, or leader. It is a form of social coexistence that all canines

recognize and accept. Discipline, therefore, is never to be confused with punishment. When you teach your puppy how you want him to behave, and he behaves properly and you praise him for it, you are disciplining him with a form of positive reinforcement.

For a dog, rewards come in the form of praise, a smile, a cheerful tone of voice, a few friendly pats or a rub of the ears. Rewards are also small food treats. Obviously, that does not mean bits of regular dog food. Instead, treats are very small bits of special things like cheese or pieces of soft dog treats. The idea is to reward the dog with something very small that he can taste and swallow, providing instant positive reinforcement. If he has to take time to chew the treat, by the time he is finished he will have forgotten what he did to earn it!

Your puppy's first pack leader was his dam. In the world of canines, mother is always right and rules the roost. Puppies pick up behavioral traits from their parents; they learn by watching (just like human kids).

You can train an adult Fox Terrier with a chain choke collar, but be sure to put it on correctly. After the training session is over, take the collar off the dog and replace it with his everyday collar and ID tag.

existence. You can try to stop it as much as you like but without success, because it's such fun for the dog. But one good hissing, spitting, swipe of a cat's claws across the dog's nose will put an end to the game forever. Intervene only when your dog's eyeball is seriously at risk. Cat scratches can cause permanent damage to an innocent but annoying puppy.

PUPPY KINDERGARTEN

COLLAR AND LEASH

Before you begin your Fox Terrier puppy's education, he must be used to his collar and leash. Choose a collar for your puppy that is secure, but not heavy or bulky. He won't enjoy training if he's uncomfortable. A flat buckle collar is fine for everyday wear

Your puppy should never be physically punished. The displeasure shown on your face and in your voice is sufficient to signal to the pup that he has done something wrong. He wants to please everyone higher up on the social ladder, especially his leader, so a scowl and harsh voice will take care of the error. Growling out the word "Shame!" when the pup is caught in the act of doing something wrong is better than the repetitive "No." Some dogs hear "No" so often that they begin to think it's their name! By the way, do not use the dog's name when you're correcting him. His name is reserved to get his attention for something pleasant about to take place.

There are punishments that have nothing to do with you. For example, your dog may think that chasing cats is one reason for his

> ### BASIC PRINCIPLES OF DOG TRAINING
> 1. Start training early. A young puppy is ready, willing and able.
> 2. Timing is your all-important tool. Praise at the exact time that the dog responds correctly. Pay close attention.
> 3. Patience is almost as important as timing!
> 4. Repeat! The same word has to mean the same thing every time.
> 5. In the beginning, praise all correct behavior verbally, along with treats and petting.

and for initial puppy training. For older dogs, there are several types of training collars such as the martingale, which is a double loop that tightens slightly around the neck, or the head collar, which is similar to a horse's halter. Do not use a chain choke collar unless you have been specifically shown how to put it on and how to use it. You may not be disposed to use a chain choke collar even if your breeder has told you that it's suitable for your Fox Terrier.

A lightweight 6-foot woven cotton or nylon training leash is preferred by most trainers because it is easy to fold up in your hand and comfortable to hold because there is a certain amount of give to it. There are lessons where the dog will start off 6 feet away from you at the end of the leash. The leash used to take the puppy outside to relieve himself is shorter because you don't want him to roam away from his area. The shorter leash will also be the one to use when you walk the puppy.

If you've been fortunate enough to enroll in a Puppy Kindergarten training class, suggestions will be made as to the best collar and leash for your young puppy. I say "fortunate" because your puppy will be in a class with puppies in his age range (up to five months old) of all breeds and sizes. It's the perfect way for him to learn the right way (and the wrong way) to interact with other dogs as well as their people. You cannot teach your puppy how to interpret another dog's sign language. For a first-time puppy owner, these socialization classes are invaluable. For experienced dog owners, they are a real boon to further training.

ATTENTION

You've been using the dog's name since the minute you collected him from the breeder, so you should be able to get his attention by saying his name—with a big smile and in an excited tone of voice. His response will be the puppy equivalent of "Here I am! What are we going to do?" Your

Check the puppy's collar every day, as he can grow a notch in no time flat. You should be able to put a finger between the puppy's neck and the collar.

The power of suggestion smells like liver! You can effectively get your dog's attention by using a food treat, accompanied by "Good dog!"

immediate response (if you haven't guessed by now) is "Good dog." Rewarding him at the moment he pays attention to you teaches him the proper way to respond when he hears his name.

EXERCISES FOR A BASIC CANINE EDUCATION

THE SIT EXERCISE

There are several ways to teach the puppy to sit. The first one is to catch him whenever he is about to sit and, as his backside nears the floor, say "Sit, good dog!" That's positive reinforcement and, if your timing is sharp, he will learn that what he's doing at that second is connected to your saying "Sit" and that you think he's clever for doing it!

Another method is to start with the puppy on his leash in front of you. Show him a treat in the palm of your right hand. Bring your hand up under his nose and, almost in slow motion, move your hand up and back so his nose goes up in the air and his head tilts back as he follows the treat in your hand. At that point, he will have to either sit or fall over, so as his back legs buckle under, say "Sit, good dog," and then give him the treat and lots of praise. You may have to begin with your hand lightly running up his chest, actually lifting his chin up until he sits. Some (usually older) dogs require gentle pressure on their

hindquarters with the left hand, in which case the dog should be on your left side. Puppies generally do not appreciate this physical dominance.

After a few times, you should be able to show the dog a treat in the open palm of your hand, raise your hand waist-high as you say "Sit" and have him sit. You will thereby have taught him two things at the same time. Both the verbal command and the motion of the hand are signals for the sit. Your puppy is watching you almost more than he is listening to you, so what you do is just as important as what you say.

Don't save any of these drills only for training sessions. Use

Always practice commands with your dog on his leash. Most trainers start with the sit exercise because it's the easiest command to master.

them as much as possible at odd times during a normal day. The dog should always sit before being given his food dish. He should sit to let you go through a doorway first, when the doorbell rings or when you stop to speak to someone on the street.

THE DOWN EXERCISE

Before beginning to teach the down command, you must consider how the dog feels about this exercise. To him, "down" is a submissive position. Being flat on the floor with you standing over him is not his idea of fun. It's up to you to let him know that, while it may not be fun, the reward of your approval is worth his effort.

SIT AROUND THE HOUSE

"Sit" is the command you'll use most often. Your pup objects when placed in a sit with your hands, so try the "bringing the food up under his chin" method. Better still, catch him in the act! Your dog will sit on his own many times throughout the day, so let him know that he's doing the "Sit" by rewarding him. Praise him and have him sit for everything—toys, connecting his leash, his dinner, before going out the door, etc.

Start with the puppy on your left side in a sit position. Hold the leash right above his collar in your left hand. Have an extra-

The stay exercise is a natural extension of the sit command. The hand signal reinforces the verbal command "Stay."

SWEET AND LOW DOWN

"Down" is a harsh-sounding word and a submissive posture in dog body language, thus presenting two obstacles in teaching the down command. When the dog is about to flop down on his own, tell him "Good down." Pups that are not good about being handled learn better by having food lowered in front of them. A dog that trusts you can be gently guided into position. When you give the command "Down," be sure to say it sweetly!

special treat, such as a small piece of cooked chicken or hot dog, in your right hand. Place it at the end of the pup's nose and steadily move your hand down and forward along the ground. Hold the leash to prevent a sudden lunge for the food. As the puppy goes into the down position, say "Down" very gently.

The difficulty with this exercise is twofold: it's both the submissive aspect and the fact that most people say the word "Down" as if they were a drill sergeant in charge of recruits! So issue the command sweetly, give him the treat and have the pup maintain the down position for several seconds. If he tries to get up immediately, place your hands on his shoulders and press down gently, giving him a very quiet "Good dog." As you progress with this lesson, increase the "down

The down exercise requires consistent training and practice. In order to have your Fox Terrier respond as flawlessly as this smart pupil, it will require concentration and commitment from you and your dog.

> ## LET'S GO!
> Many people use "Let's go" instead of "Heel" when teaching their dogs to behave on lead. It sounds more like fun! When beginning to teach the heel, whatever command you use, always step off on your left foot. That's the one next to the dog, who is on your left side, in case you've forgotten. Keep a loose leash. When the dog pulls ahead, stop, bring him back and begin again. Use treats to guide him around turns.

time" until he will hold it until you say "Okay" (his cue for release). Practice this one in the house at various times throughout the day.

By increasing the length of time during which the dog must maintain the down position, you'll find many uses for it. For

example, he can lie at your feet in the vet's office or anywhere that both of you have to wait, when you are on the phone, while the family is eating and so forth. If you progress to training for competitive obedience, he'll already be all set for the exercise called the "long down."

THE STAY EXERCISE

You can teach your Fox Terrier to stay in the sit, down and stand positions. To teach the sit/stay, have the dog sit on your left side. Hold the leash at waist level in your left hand and let the dog know that you have a treat in your closed right hand. Step forward on your right foot as you say "Stay." Immediately turn and stand directly in front of the dog, keeping your right hand up high so he'll keep his eye on the treat

Fox Terriers love to follow their masters, which makes teaching the stay a little more difficult. As your dog's trainer, you have to act as if you know what you're doing (even if you have to fake it for the first few lessons). Give him a trainer he can trust. Owner, Joanne Pongones.

hand and maintain the sit position for a count of five. Return to your original position and offer the reward.

Increase the length of the sit/stay each time until the dog can hold it for at least 30 seconds without moving. After about a week of success, move out on your right foot and take two steps before turning to face the dog. Give the "Stay" hand signal (left palm back toward the dog's head) as you leave. He gets the treat when you return and he holds the sit/stay. Increase the distance that you walk away from him before turning until you reach the length of your training leash. But don't rush it! Go back to the beginning if he moves before he should. No matter what the lesson, never be upset by having to back up for a few days. The repetition and practice are what will make your dog reliable in these commands. It won't do any good to move on to something more difficult if the command is not mastered at the easier levels. Above all, even if you do get frustrated, never let your puppy know! Always keep a positive, upbeat attitude during training, which will transmit to your dog for positive results.

The down/stay is taught in the same way once the dog is completely reliable and steady with the down command. Again, don't rush it. With the dog in the down position on your left side,

> ### OKAY!
> This is the signal that tells your dog that he can quit whatever he was doing. Use "Okay" to end a session on a correct response to a command. (Never end on an incorrect response.) Lots of praise follows. People use "Okay" a lot and it has other uses for dogs, too. Your dog is barking. You say, "Okay! Come!" "Okay" signals him to stop the barking activity and "Come" allows him to come to you for a "Good dog."

step out on your right foot as you say "Stay." Return by walking around in back of the dog and into your original position. While you are training, it's okay to murmur something like "Hold on" to encourage him to stay put. When the dog will stay without moving when you are at a distance of 3 or 4 feet, begin to increase the length of time before you return. Be sure he holds the down on your return until you say "Okay." At that point, he gets his treat—just so he'll remember for next time that it's not over until it's over.

THE COME EXERCISE
No command is more important to the safety of your Fox Terrier than "come." It is what you should say every single time you see the puppy running toward you: "Binky, come! Good dog." During playtime, run a few feet away

from the puppy and turn and tell him to "come" as he is already running to you. You can go so far as to teach your puppy two things at once if you squat down and hold out your arms. As the pup gets close to you and you're saying "Good dog," bring your right arm in about waist high. Now he's also learning the hand signal, an excellent device should you be on the phone when you

Practice the come command on leash. Your Fox Terrier will happily return to you for a treat or some hearty praise.

COME AND GET IT!
The come command is your dog's safety signal. Until he is 99% perfect in responding, don't use the come command if you cannot enforce it. Practice on leash with treats or squeakers, or whenever the dog is running to you. Never call him to come to you if he is to be corrected for a misdemeanor. Reward the dog with a treat and happy praise whenever he comes to you.

need to get him to come to you! You'll also both be one step ahead when you enter obedience classes.

Puppies, like children, have notoriously short attention spans, so don't overdo it with any of the training. Keep each lesson short. Break it up with a quick run around the yard or a ball toss, repeat the lesson and quit as soon as the pup gets it right. That way, you will always end with a "Good dog."

When the puppy responds to your well-timed "Come," try it with the puppy on the training leash. This time, catch him off guard, while he's sniffing a leaf or watching a bird: "Binky, come!" You may have to pause for a split second after his name to be sure you have his attention. If the puppy shows any sign of confusion, give the leash a mild jerk and take a couple of steps backward. Do not repeat the command. In this case, you should say "Good come" as he reaches you.

That's the number-one rule of training. Each command word is given just once. Anything more is nagging. You'll also notice that all commands are one word only. Even when they are actually two words, you say them as one.

Never call the dog to come to you—with or without his name—if you are angry or intend to correct him for some misbehavior. When correcting the pup, you go to him. Your dog must always connect "come" with something pleasant and with your approval; then you can rely on his response.

Life isn't perfect and neither are puppies. A time will come, often around 10 months of age, when he'll become "selectively deaf" or choose to "forget" his name. He may respond by wagging his tail (and even

Heeling requires your Fox Terrier to move at your left side at your pace. This lesson has practical applications in your everyday life: a dog that heels well is a pleasure to walk and looks like a million bucks.

seeming to smile at you) with a look that says "Make me!" Laugh, throw his favorite toy and skip the lesson you had planned. Pups will be pups!

THE HEEL EXERCISE

The second most important command to teach, after the come, is the heel. When you are walking your growing puppy, you need to be in control. Besides, it looks terrible to be pulled and yanked down the street, and it's not much fun either. Your eight-to ten-week-old puppy will probably follow you everywhere, but that's his natural instinct, not your control over the situation. However, any time he does follow you, you can say "Heel" and be ahead of the

I WILL FOLLOW YOU

Obedience isn't just a classroom activity. In your home you have many great opportunities to teach your dog polite manners. Allowing your pet on the bed or furniture elevates him to your level, which is not a good idea (the word is "Off!"). Use the "umbilical cord" method, keeping your dog on lead so he has to go with you wherever you go. You sit, he sits. You walk, he heels. You stop, he sit-stays. Everywhere you go, he's with you, but you go first!

game, as he will learn to associate this command with the action of following you before you even begin teaching him to heel.

There is a very precise, almost military, procedure for teaching your dog to heel. As with all other obedience training, begin with the dog on your left side. He will be in a very nice sit and you will have the training leash across your chest. Hold the loop and folded leash in your right hand. Pick up the slack leash above the dog in your left hand and hold it loosely at your side. Step out on your left foot as you say "Heel." If the puppy does not move, give a gentle tug or pat your left leg to get him started. If he surges ahead of you, stop and pull him back

> ### "COME" . . . BACK
> Never call your dog to come to you for a correction or scold him when he reaches you. That is the quickest way to turn a come command into "Go away fast!" Dogs think only in the present tense, and your dog will connect the scolding with coming to you, not with the misbehavior of a few moments earlier.

gently until he is at your side. Tell him to sit and begin again.

Walk a few steps and stop while the puppy is correctly beside you. Tell him to sit and give mild verbal praise. (More enthusiastic praise will encourage him to think the lesson is over.) Repeat the lesson, increasing the number of steps you take only as long as the dog is heeling nicely beside you. When you end the lesson, have him hold the sit, then give him the "Okay" to let him know that this is the end of the lesson. Praise him so that he knows he did a good job.

The cure for excessive pulling (a common problem) is to stop when the dog is no more than 2 or 3 feet ahead of you. Guide him back into position and begin again. With a really determined puller, try switching to a head collar. This will automatically turn the pup's head toward you so you can bring him back easily to the heel position. Give quiet, reassuring praise every time the

In the heel exercise, your Fox Terrier should sit whenever you come to a complete stop. This is a real advantage when approaching an intersection with your dog (unless, of course, there's a puddle!).

leash goes slack and he's staying with you.

Staying and heeling can take a lot out of a dog, so provide playtime and free-running exercise to shake off the stress when the lessons are over. You don't want him to associate training with all work and no fun.

RIGHT CLICK ON YOUR DOG

With three clicks, the dolphin jumps through the hoop. Wouldn't it be nice to have a dog who could obey wordless commands that easily? Clicker training actually was developed by dolphin trainers and today is used on dogs with great success. You can buy a clicker at a pet shop or pet-supply outlet, and then you'll be off and clicking.

You can click your dog into learning new commands, shaping or conditioning his behavior and solving bad habits. The clicker, used in conjunction with a treat, is an extension of positive reinforcement. The dog begins to recognize your happy clicking, and you will never have to use physical force again. The dog is conditioned to follow your hand with the clicker, just as he would follow your hand with a treat. To discourage the dog from inappropriate behavior (like jumping up or barking), you can use the clicker to set a timeframe and then click and reward the dog once he's waited the allotted time without jumping up or barking.

Most Fox Terriers will dance at the slightest whiff of liver. Your ultimate goal is to make him dance without a treat: fox trot, anyone?

TAPERING OFF TIDBITS

Your dog has been watching you—and the hand that treats—throughout all of his lessons, and now it's time to break the treat habit. Begin by giving him treats at the end of each lesson only. Then start to give a treat after the end of only some of the lessons. At the end of every lesson, as well as during the lessons, be consistent with the praise. Your pup now doesn't know whether he'll get a treat or not, but he should keep performing well just in case! Finally, you will stop giving treat rewards entirely. Save them for something brand-new that you want to teach him. Keep up the praise and you'll always have a "good dog."

OBEDIENCE CLASSES

The advantages of an obedience class are that your dog will have to learn amid the distractions of other people and dogs and that your mistakes will be quickly corrected by the trainer. Teaching your dog along with a qualified instructor and other handlers who may have more dog experience than you is another plus of the class environment. The instructor and other handlers can help you

In the training of a show dog, luring the dog with food is called baiting.

> ### MORE PRAISE, LESS FOOD
> As you progress with your puppy's lessons, and the puppy is responding well, gradually begin to wean him off the treats by alternating the treats with times when you offer only verbal praise or a few pats on the dog's side. (Pats on the head are dominant actions, so he won't think they are meant to be praise.) Every lesson should end with the puppy's performing the correct action for that session's command. When he gets it right and you withhold the treat, the praise can be as long and lavish as you like. The commands are one word only, but your verbal praise can use as many words as you want...don't skimp!

to find the most efficient way of teaching your dog a command or exercise. It's often easier to learn by other people's mistakes than your own. You will also learn all of the requirements for competitive obedience trials, in which you can earn titles and go on to advanced jumping and retrieving exercises, which are fun for many dogs. Obedience classes build the foundation needed for many other canine activities (in which we humans are allowed to participate, too!).

TRAINING FOR OTHER ACTIVITIES

Once your dog has basic obedience under his collar and is

12 months of age, you can enter the world of agility training. Dogs think agility is pure fun, like being turned loose in an amusement park full of obstacles! In addition to agility, there are hunting activities for sporting dogs, lure-coursing events for sighthounds, go-to-ground events for terriers, racing for the Nordic sled dogs, herding trials for the shepherd breeds and tracking, which is open to all "nosey" dogs (which would include all dogs!). For those who like to volunteer, there is the wonderful feeling of owning a therapy dog and visiting hospices, nursing homes and veterans' homes to bring smiles, comfort and companionship to

HOW DO I GET TO CARNEGIE HALL?

Or the National Obedience Championships? The same way you get your dog to do anything else—practice, practice, practice. It's *how* you practice that counts. Keep sessions short, varied, interesting and interspersed with active fun. A bored dog isn't learning. If you're feeling out of sorts yourself, quit for the day. Set yourself a reasonable schedule for several brief practice sessions every day and stick to it. Practice randomly throughout the day as you're doing different things around the house. Lots of praise for that good "Sit" in front of the TV or while waiting for his dinner!

those who live there.

Around the house, your Fox Terrier can be taught to do some simple chores. You might teach him to carry a basket of household items or to fetch the morning newspaper. The kids can teach the dog all kinds of tricks, from playing hide-and-seek to balancing a biscuit on his nose. A family dog is what rounds out the family. Everything he does beyond sitting in your lap or gazing lovingly at you represents the bonus of owning a dog.

High flying, adored: a Fox Terrier in flight at an agility trial is a sight to behold. Given the natural agility and intelligence of the Fox Terrier, agility trials are a great venue for the breed to show off its talents.

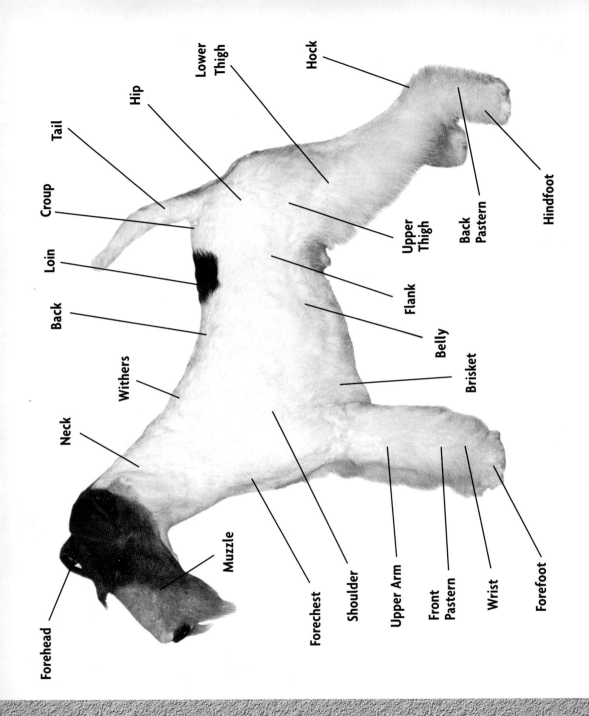

Lower Thigh

Hock

Hip

Tail

Croup

Upper Thigh

Back Pastern

Hindfoot

Loin

Back

Flank

Withers

Belly

Neck

Brisket

Muzzle

Forechest

Shoulder

Upper Arm

Front Pastern

Wrist

Forefoot

Forehead

PHYSICAL STRUCTURE OF THE FOX TERRIER

HEALTHCARE OF YOUR

FOX TERRIER

By Lowell Ackerman DVM, DACVD

HEALTHCARE FOR A LIFETIME
When you own a dog, you become his healthcare advocate over his entire lifespan, as well as being the one to shoulder the financial burden of such care. Accordingly, it is worthwhile to focus on prevention rather than treatment, as you and your pet will both be happier.

Of course, the best place to have begun your program of preventive healthcare is with the initial purchase or adoption of your dog. There is no way of guaranteeing that your new furry friend is free of medical problems, but there are some things you can do to improve your odds. You certainly should have done adequate research into the Fox Terrier and have selected your puppy carefully rather than buying on impulse. Health issues aside, a large number of pet abandonment and relinquishment cases arise from a mismatch between pet needs and owner expectations. This is entirely preventable with appropriate planning and finding a good breeder.

Regarding healthcare issues specifically, it is very difficult to make blanket statements about where to acquire a problem-free pet, but, again, a reputable breeder is your best bet. In an ideal situation you have the opportunity to see both parents, get references from other owners of the breeder's pups and see genetic-testing documentation for several generations of the litter's ancestors. At the very least, you must thoroughly investigate the Fox Terrier and the problems inherent in that breed, as well as the genetic testing available to screen for those problems. Genetic testing offers some important benefits, but testing is available for only a few disorders in a relatively small number of breeds and is not available for some of the most common genetic diseases, such as hip dysplasia, cataracts, epilepsy, cardiomyopathy, etc. This area of research is indeed exciting and increasingly important, and advances will continue to be made each year. In fact, recent research has shown that there is an equivalent dog gene for 75% of known human genes, so research done in

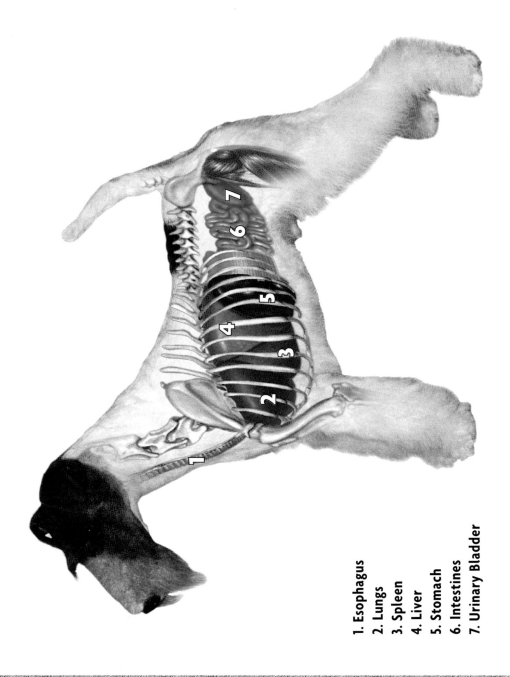

1. Esophagus
2. Lungs
3. Spleen
4. Liver
5. Stomach
6. Intestines
7. Urinary Bladder

INTERNAL ORGANS OF THE FOX TERRIER

either species is likely to benefit the other.

We've also discussed that evaluating the behavioral nature of your Fox Terrier and that of his immediate family members is an important part of the selection process that cannot be underestimated or underemphasized. It is sometimes difficult to evaluate temperament in puppies because certain behavioral tendencies, such as some forms of aggression, may not be immediately evident. More dogs are euthanized each year for behavioral reasons than for all medical conditions combined, so it is critical to take temperament issues seriously. Start with a well-balanced, friendly companion and put the time and effort into proper socialization, and you will both be rewarded with a lifelong valued relationship.

Assuming that you have started off with a pup from healthy, sound stock, you then become responsible for helping your veterinarian keep your pet healthy. Some crucial things happen before you even bring your puppy home. Parasite control typically begins at two weeks of age, and vaccinations typically begin at six to eight weeks of age. A pre-pubertal evaluation is typically scheduled for about six months of age. At this time, a dental evaluation is done (since the adult teeth are

now in), heartworm prevention is started and neutering or spaying is most commonly done.

It is critical to commence regular dental care at home if you have not already done so. It may not sound very important, but most dogs have active periodontal disease by four years of age if they don't have their teeth cleaned regularly at home, not just at their veterinary exams. Dental problems lead to more than just bad "doggie breath": gum disease can have very serious medical consequences. If you start brushing your dog's teeth and using antiseptic rinses from a young age, your dog will be accustomed to it and will not resist. The results will be healthy dentition, which your pet will need to enjoy a long, healthy life.

Most dogs are considered adults at a year of age, although some larger breeds still have some filling out to do up to about two or so years old. Even individual dogs within each breed have different healthcare requirements, so work with your veterinarian to determine what will be needed and what your role should be. This doctor-client relationship is important, because as vaccination guidelines change, there may not be an annual "vaccine visit" scheduled. You must make sure that you see your veterinarian at least annually, even if no vaccines are due, because this is the best

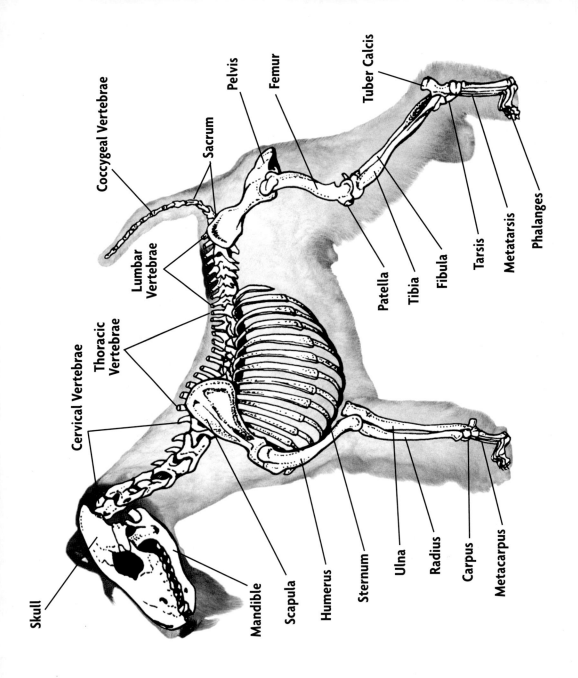

Skeletal Structure of the Fox Terrier

opportunity to coordinate health-care activities and to make sure that no medical issues creep by unaddressed.

When your Fox Terrier reaches three-quarters of his anticipated lifespan, he is considered a "senior" and likely requires some special care. In general, if you've been taking great care of your canine companion throughout his formative and adult years, the transition to senior status should be a smooth one. Age is not a disease, and as long as everything is functioning as it should, there is no reason why most of late adulthood should not be rewarding for both you and your pet. This is especially true if you have tended to the details, such as regular veterinary visits, proper dental care, excellent nutrition and management of bone and joint issues.

Before socialization with other puppies can begin, ensure that your puppy has been properly inoculated.

At this stage in your Fox Terrier's life, your veterinarian may want to schedule visits twice yearly, instead of once, to run some laboratory screenings, electrocardiograms and the like, and to change the diet to something more digestible. Catching problems early is the best way to manage them effectively. Treating the early stages of heart disease is so much easier than trying to intervene when there is more significant damage to the heart muscle. Similarly, managing the beginning of kidney problems is fairly routine if there is no significant kidney damage. Other problems, like cognitive dysfunction (similar to senility and Alzheimer's disease), cancer, diabetes and arthritis, are more common in older dogs, but all can be treated to help the dog live as many happy, comfortable years as possible. Just as in people, medical management is more effective (and less expensive) when you catch things early.

PUPPY PARASITES

Parasites are nasty little critters that live in or on your dog or puppy. Most puppies are born with ascarid roundworms, which are acquired from dormant ascarids residing in the dam. Other parasites can be acquired through contact with infected fecal matter. Take a stool sample to your vet for testing. He will prescribe a safe wormer to treat any parasites found in your puppy's stool. Always have a fecal test performed at your puppy's annual veterinary exam.

SELECTING A VETERINARIAN

There is probably no more important decision that you will make regarding your pet's health-care than the selection of his doctor. Your pet's veterinarian will be a pediatrician, family-practice physician and gerontologist, depending on the dog's life stage, and will be the individual who makes recommendations regarding issues such as when specialists need to be consulted, when diagnostic testing and/or therapeutic intervention is needed and when you will need to seek outside emergency and critical-care services. Your vet will act as your advocate and liaison throughout these processes.

Everyone has his own idea about what to look for in a vet, an individual who will play a big role in his dog's (and, of course, his own) life for many years to come. For some, it is the compassionate caregiver with whom they hope to develop a professional relationship to span the lifetime of their dogs and even their future pets. For others, they are seeking a clinician with keen diagnostic and therapeutic insight who can deliver state-of-the-art healthcare. Still others need a veterinary facility that is open evenings and weekends, or is in close proximity or provides mobile veterinary services, to accommodate their schedules; these people may not much mind that their dogs might

see different veterinarians on each visit. Just as we have different reasons for selecting our own healthcare professionals (e.g.,

---

YOUR DOG NEEDS TO VISIT THE VET IF:

- He has ingested a toxin such as antifreeze or a toxic plant; in these cases, administer first aid and call the vet right away
- His teeth are discolored, loose or missing or he has sores or other signs of infection or abnormality in the mouth
- He has been vomiting, has had diarrhea or has been constipated for over 24 hours; call immediately if you notice blood
- He has refused food for over 24 hours
- His eating habits, water intake or toilet habits have noticeably changed; if you have noticed weight gain or weight loss
- He shows symptoms of bloat, which requires *immediate* attention
- He is salivating excessively
- He has a lump in his throat
- He has a lump or bumps anywhere on the body
- He is very lethargic
- He appears to be in pain or otherwise has trouble chewing or swallowing
- His skin loses elasticity.

Of course, there will be other instances in which a visit to the vet is necessary; these are just some of the signs that could be indicative of serious problems that need to be caught as early as possible.

covered by insurance plan, expert in field, convenient location, etc.), we should not expect that there is a one-size-fits-all recommendation for selecting a veterinarian and veterinary practice. The best advice is to be honest in your assessment of what you expect from a veterinary practice and to conscientiously research the options in your area. You will quickly appreciate that not all veterinary practices are the same, and you will be happiest with one that truly meets your needs.

There is another point to be considered in the selection of veterinary services. Not that long ago, a single veterinarian would attempt to manage all medical and surgical issues as they arose. That was often problematic, because veterinarians are trained in many species and many diseases, and it was just impossible for general veterinary practitioners to be experts in every species, every field and every ailment. However, just as in the human healthcare fields, specialization has allowed general practitioners to concentrate on primary healthcare delivery, especially wellness and the prevention of infectious diseases, and to utilize a network of specialists to assist in the management of conditions that require specific expertise and

SAMPLE VACCINATION SCHEDULE

6–8 weeks of age	Parvovirus, Distemper, Adenovirus-2 (Hepatitis)
9–11 weeks of age	Parvovirus, Distemper, Adenovirus-2 (Hepatitis)
12–14 weeks of age	Parvovirus, Distemper, Adenovirus-2 (Hepatitis)
16–20 weeks of age	Rabies
1 year of age	Parvovirus, Distemper, Adenovirus-2 (Hepatitis), Rabies

Revaccination is performed every one to three years, depending on the product, the method of administration and the patient's risk. Initial adult inoculation (for dogs at least 16 weeks of age in which a puppy series was not done or could not be confirmed) is two vaccinations, done three to four weeks apart, with revaccination according to the same criteria mentioned. Other vaccines are given as decided between owner and veterinarian.

COMMON INFECTIOUS DISEASES

Let's discuss some of the diseases that create the need for vaccination in the first place. Following are the major canine infectious diseases and a simple explanation of each.

Rabies: A devastating viral disease that can be fatal in dogs and people. In fact, vaccination of dogs and cats is an important public-health measure to create a resistant animal buffer population to protect people from contracting the disease. Vaccination schedules are determined on a government level and are not optional for pet owners; rabies vaccination is required by law in all 50 states.

Parvovirus: A severe, potentially life-threatening disease that is easily transmitted between dogs. There are four strains of the virus, but it is believed that there is significant "cross-protection" between strains that may be included in individual vaccines.

Distemper: A potentially severe and life-threatening disease with a relatively high risk of exposure, especially in certain regions. In very high-risk distemper environments, young pups may be vaccinated with human measles vaccine, a related virus that offers cross-protection when administered at four to ten weeks of age.

Hepatitis: Caused by canine adenovirus type 1 (CAV-1), but since vaccination with the causative virus has a higher rate of adverse effects, cross-protection is derived from the use of adenovirus type 2 (CAV-2), a cause of respiratory disease and one of the potential causes of canine cough. Vaccination with CAV-2 provides long-term immunity against hepatitis, but relatively less protection against respiratory infection.

Canine cough: Also called tracheobronchitis, actually a fairly complicated result of viral and bacterial offenders; therefore, even with vaccination, protection is incomplete. Wherever dogs congregate, canine cough will likely be spread among them. Intranasal vaccination with *Bordetella* and parainfluenza is the best safeguard, but the duration of immunity does not appear to be very long, typically a year at most. These are non-core vaccines, but vaccination is sometimes mandated by boarding kennels, obedience classes, dog shows and other places where dogs congregate to try to minimize spread of infection.

Leptospirosis: A potentially fatal disease that is more common in some geographic regions. It is capable of being spread to humans. The disease varies with the individual "serovar," or strain, of *Leptospira* involved. Since there does not appear to be much cross-protection between serovars, protection is only as good as the likelihood that the serovar in the vaccine is the same as the one in the pet's local environment. Problems with *Leptospira* vaccines are that protection does not last very long, side effects are not uncommon and a large percentage of dogs (perhaps 30%) may not respond to vaccination.

Borrelia burgdorferi: The cause of Lyme disease, the risk of which varies with the geographic area in which the pet lives and travels. Lyme disease is spread by deer ticks in the eastern US and western black-legged ticks in the western part of the country, and the risk of exposure is high in some regions. Lameness, fever and inappetence are most commonly seen in affected dogs. The extent of protection from the vaccine has not been conclusively demonstrated.

Coronavirus: This disease has a high risk of exposure, especially in areas where dogs congregate, but it typically causes only mild to moderate digestive upset (diarrhea, vomiting, etc.). Vaccines are available, but the duration of protection is believed to be relatively short and the effectiveness of the vaccine in preventing infection is considered low.

There are many other vaccinations available, including those for *Giardia* and canine adenovirus-1. While there may be some specific indications for their use, and local risk factors to be considered, they are not widely recommended for most dogs.

experience. Thus there are now many types of veterinary specialists, including dermatologists, cardiologists, ophthalmologists, surgeons, internists, oncologists, neurologists, behaviorists, criticalists and others to help primary-care veterinarians deal with complicated medical challenges. In most cases, specialists see cases referred by primary-care veterinarians, make diagnoses and set up management plans. From there, the animals' ongoing care is returned to their primary-care veterinarians. This important team approach to your pet's medical-care needs has provided opportunities for advanced care and an unparalleled level of quality to be delivered.

With all of the opportunities for your Fox Terrier to receive high-quality veterinary medical care, there is another topic that needs to be addressed at the same time—cost. It's been said that you can have excellent healthcare or inexpensive healthcare, but never both; this is as true in veterinary medicine as it is in human medicine. While veterinary costs are a fraction of what the same services cost in the human health-care arena, it is still difficult to deal with unanticipated medical costs, especially since they can easily creep into hundreds or even thousands of dollars if specialists or emergency services become involved. However, there

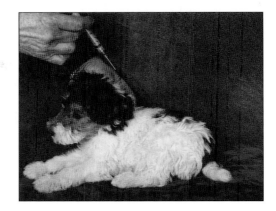

are ways of managing these risks. The easiest is to buy pet health insurance and realize that its foremost purpose is not to cover routine healthcare visits but rather to serve as an umbrella for those rainy days when your pet needs medical care and you don't want to worry about whether or not you can afford that care.

Pet insurance policies are very cost-effective (and very inexpensive by human health-insurance standards), but make sure that you buy the policy long before you intend to use it (preferably starting in puppyhood, because coverage will exclude pre-existing conditions) and that you are actually buying an indemnity insurance plan from an insurance company that is regulated by your state or province. Many insurance policy look-alikes are actually discount clubs that are redeemable only at specific locations and for specific services. An indemnity plan covers your pet at

Vaccinations protect puppies from the common infectious diseases that can kill or debilitate dogs. Discuss and plan an inoculation schedule with your veterinarian at the first visit to his office.

almost all veterinary, specialty and emergency practices and is an excellent way to manage your pet's ongoing healthcare needs.

VACCINATIONS AND INFECTIOUS DISEASES

There has never been an easier time to prevent a variety of infectious diseases in your dog, but the advances we've made in veterinary medicine come with a price—choice. Now while it may seem that choice is a good thing (and it is), it has never been more difficult for the pet owner (or the veterinarian) to make an informed decision about the best way to protect pets through vaccination.

Years ago, it was just accepted that puppies got a starter series of vaccinations and then annual "boosters" throughout their lives to keep them protected. As more and more vaccines became available, consumers wanted the convenience of having all of that protection in a single injection. The result was "multivalent" vaccines that crammed a lot of protection into a single syringe. The manufacturers' recommendations were to give the vaccines annually, and this was a simple enough protocol to follow. However, as veterinary medicine has become more sophisticated and we have started looking more at healthcare quandaries rather than convenience, it became necessary to reevaluate the

situation and deal with some tough questions. It is important to realize that whether or not to use a particular vaccine depends on the risk of contracting the disease against which it protects, the severity of the disease if it is contracted, the duration of immunity provided by the vaccine, the safety of the product and the needs of the individual animal. In a very general sense, rabies, distemper, hepatitis and parvovirus are considered core vaccine needs, while parainfluenza, *Bordetella bronchiseptica*, leptospirosis, coronavirus and borreliosis (Lyme

ARE VACCINATIONS NECESSARY?

Vaccinations are recommended for all puppies by the American Veterinary Medical Association (AVMA). Some vaccines are absolutely necessary, while others depend upon a dog's or puppy's individual exposure to certain diseases or the animal's immune history. Rabies vaccinations are required by law in all 50 states. Some diseases are fatal whereas others are treatable, making the need for vaccinating against the latter questionable. Follow your veterinarian's recommendations to keep your dog fully immunized and protected. You can also review the AVMA directive on vaccinations on their website: www.avma.org.

OPPOSITE: From early puppyhood through the senior years, your Fox Terrier relies upon you for his complete healthcare. It's your responsibility to be a well-informed canine guardian and keeper.

disease) are considered non-core needs and best reserved for animals that demonstrate reasonable risk of contracting the diseases.

THE GREAT VACCINATION DEBATE

What kinds of questions need to be addressed? When the vet injects multiple organisms at the same time, might some of the components interfere with one another in the development of immunologic protection? We don't have the comprehensive answer for that question, but it does appear that the immune system better handles agents when given individually. Unfortunately, most manufacturers still bundle their vaccine components because that is what most pet owners want, so getting vaccines with single components can sometimes be difficult.

Your puppy should have received two, possibly three, sets of inoculations before you bring him home.

Another question has to do with how often vaccines should be given. Again, this seems to be different for each vaccine component. There seems to be a general consensus that a puppy (or a dog with an unknown vaccination history) should get a series of vaccinations to initially stimulate his immunity and then a booster at one year of age, but even the veterinary associations and colleges have trouble reaching agreement about what he should get after that. Rabies vaccination schedules are not debated, because vaccine schedules for this contagious and devastating disease are determined by government agencies. Regarding the rest, some recommend that we continue to give the vaccines annually because this method has worked well as a disease preventive for decades and delivers predictable protection. Others recommend that some of the vaccines need to be given only every second or third year, as this can be done without affecting levels of protection. This is probably true for some vaccine components (such as hepatitis), but there have been no large studies to demonstrate what the optimal interval should be and whether the same principles hold true for all breeds.

It may be best to just measure titers, which are protective blood levels of various vaccine components, on an annual basis, but that too is not without controversy. Scientists have not precisely determined the minimum titer of specific vaccine components that will be guaranteed to provide a pet with protection. Pets with very high titers will clearly be protected and those with very low titers will need repeat vaccinations, but there is also a large "gray zone" of pets that probably have intermediate protection and may or may not need repeat vaccination, depending on their risk of coming into contact with the disease.

These questions leave primary-care veterinarians in a very uncomfortable position, one that is not easy to resolve. Do they recommend annual vaccination in a manner that has demonstrated successful protection for decades, do they recommend skipping vaccines some years and hope that the protection lasts or do they measure blood tests (titers) and hope that the results are convincing enough to clearly indicate whether repeat vaccination is warranted?

These aren't the only vaccination questions impacting pets, owners and veterinarians. Other controversies focus on whether vaccines should be dosed according to body weight (currently they are administered in uniform doses, regardless of the animal's size), whether there are

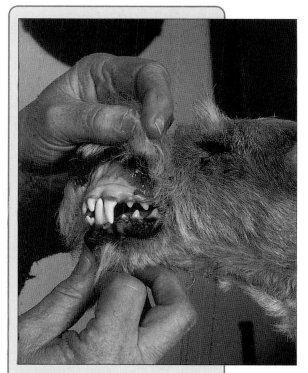

DENTAL HEALTH

A dental examination is in order when the dog is between six months and one year of age so that any permanent teeth that have erupted incorrectly can be corrected. It is important to begin a brushing routine. Durable nylon and safe edible chews should be a part of your puppy's arsenal for good health, good teeth and pleasant breath. The vast majority of dogs three to four years old and older have diseases of the gums from lack of dental attention. Using the various types of dental chews can be very effective in controlling dental plaque.

breed-specific issues important in determining vaccination programs (for instance, we know that some breeds have a harder time mounting an appropriate immune response to parvovirus vaccine and might benefit from a different dose or injection interval) and which type of vaccine—live-virus or inactivated—offers more advantages with fewer disadvantages. Clearly, there are many more questions than there are answers. The important thing, as a pet owner, is to be aware of the issues and be able to work with your veterinarian to make decisions that are right for your pet. Be an informed consumer and you will appreciate the deliberation required in tailoring a vaccination program to best meet the needs of your pet. Expect also that this is an ongoing, ever-changing topic of debate; thus, the decisions you make this year won't necessarily be the same as the ones you make next year.

"Apples make me itch!" Dogs can be allergic to any food, including fruits, grains and meats.

NEUTERING/SPAYING

Sterilization procedures (neutering for males/spaying for females) are meant to accomplish several purposes. While the underlying premise is to address the risk of pet overpopulation, there are also some medical and behavioral benefits to the surgeries as well. For females, spaying prior to the first estrus (heat cycle) leads to a marked reduction in the risk of mammary

The family cat acts as the surrogate dam while the real mom takes a break from her duties.

cancer. There also will be no manifestations of "heat" to attract male dogs and no bleeding in the house. For males, there is prevention of testicular cancer and a reduction in the risk of prostate problems. In both sexes there may be some limited reduction in aggressive behaviors toward other dogs, and some diminishing of urine marking, roaming and mounting.

While neutering and spaying do indeed prevent animals from contributing to pet overpopulation, even no-cost and low-cost neutering options have not eliminated the problem. Perhaps one of the main reasons for this is that individuals that intentionally breed their dogs and those that allow their animals to run at large are the main causes of unwanted

---

PSEUDOPREGNANCY

Your female dog can experience a pseudopregnancy if she is not bred during her estrous cycle. This pseudocyesis usually occurs about eight weeks after her period and is accompanied by swollen mammary glands and an enlarged abdomen. Your bitch may "adopt" one of her toys as her litter and demonstrate nesting behavior (digging a burrow in your couch or her bed). She may also exhibit aggressive behavior toward humans who attempt to threaten her "litter."

Pseudocyesis may trace back to wolf behavior in the wild. Commonly the aunts or granddam of a litter will assist another bitch in the pack with her litter. All of the bitches will feed the pups and protect them.

Since there are health risks involved with pseudopregnancy, owners are advised to spay their bitches to prevent a recurrence. Bitches can suffer from uterine infections, which can threaten their lives.

In warm weather, your Fox Terrier needs to have shade and plenty of water. Heat stroke claims the lives of many dogs during the summer months.

offspring. Also, animals in shelters are often there because they were abandoned or relinquished, not because they came from unplanned matings. Neutering/spaying is important, but it should be considered in the context of the real causes of animals' ending up in shelters and eventually being euthanized.

One of the important consid-erations regarding neutering is that it is a surgical procedure. This sometimes gets lost in discussions of low-cost procedures and commoditization of the process. In females, spaying is specifically referred to as an ovariohysterectomy. In this procedure, a midline incision is made in the abdomen and the entire uterus and both ovaries are surgically removed. While this is a major invasive surgical procedure, it usually has few complications, because it is typically performed on healthy young animals. However, it is major surgery, as any woman who has had a hysterectomy will attest.

In males, neutering has traditionally referred to castration, which involves the surgical removal of both testicles. While still a significant piece of surgery, there is not the abdominal exposure that is required in the female surgery. In addition, there is now a chemical sterilization option, in which a solution is injected into each testicle, leading to atrophy of the sperm-producing cells. This can typically be done under sedation rather than full anesthesia. This is a relatively new approach, and there are no long-term clinical studies yet available.

Neutering/spaying is typically done around six months of age at most veterinary hospitals, although techniques have been pioneered to perform the procedures in animals as young as eight weeks of age. In general, the surgeries on the very young animals are done for the specific reason of sterilizing them before they go to their new homes. This is done in some shelter hospitals for assurance that the animals will definitely not produce any pups. Otherwise, these organizations need to rely on owners to comply with their wishes to have the animals "altered" at a later date, something that does not always happen.

There are some exciting immunocontraceptive "vaccines" currently under development, and there may be a time when contraception in pets will not require surgical procedures. We anxiously await these developments.

There's no mistaking that Fox Terrier smile! Keep your Fox Terrier happy and healthy by knowing his daily signs of wellness, visiting the veterinarian annually, spaying/neutering your pet and keeping his inoculations up to date.

S. E. M. by Dr. Dennis Kunkel, University of Hawaii

A scanning electron micrograph of a dog flea, *Ctenocephalides canis*, on dog hair.

EXTERNAL PARASITES

FLEAS

Fleas have been around for millions of years and, while we have better tools now for controlling them than at any time in the past, there still is little chance that they will end up on an endangered species list. Actually, they are very well adapted to living on our pets, and they continue to adapt as we make advances.

The female flea can consume 15 times her weight in blood during active reproduction and can lay as many as 40 eggs a day. These eggs are very resistant to the effects of insecticides. They hatch into larvae, which then mature and spin cocoons. The immature fleas reside in this pupal stage until the time is right for feeding. This pupal stage is also very resistant to the effects of insecticides, and pupae can last in the environment without feeding for many months. Newly emergent fleas are attracted to animals by the warmth of the animals' bodies, movement and exhaled carbon dioxide. However, when they first emerge from their cocoons, they orient towards light; thus when an animal passes between a flea and the light source, casting a shadow, the flea pounces and starts to feed. If the animal turns out to be a dog or cat, the reproductive cycle continues. If the flea lands on another type of animal, including a person, the flea will bite but will then look for a more appropriate host. An emerging adult flea can survive without feeding for up to 12 months but, once it tastes blood, it can survive off its host for only three to four days.

It was once thought that fleas spend most of their lives in the environment, but we now know that fleas won't willingly jump off a dog unless leaping to another dog or when physically removed by brushing, bathing or other manipulation. Flea eggs, on the other hand, are shiny and smooth, and they roll off the animal and into the environment. The eggs, larvae and pupae then exist in the environment, but once the adult finds a susceptible animal, it's home sweet home until the flea is forced to seek refuge elsewhere.

Since adult fleas live on the animal and immature forms survive in the environment, a successful treatment plan must address all stages of the flea life cycle. There are now several safe and effective flea-control products that can be applied on a monthly

> ### FLEA PREVENTION FOR YOUR DOG
> - Discuss with your veterinarian the safest product to protect your dog, likely in the form of a monthly tablet or a liquid preparation placed on the back of the dog's neck.
> - For dogs suffering from flea-bite dermatitis, a shampoo or topical insecticide treatment is required.
> - Your lawn and property should be sprayed with an insecticide designed to kill fleas and ticks that lurk outdoors.
> - Using a flea comb, check the dog's coat regularly for any signs of parasites.
> - Practice good housekeeping. Vacuum floors, carpets and furniture regularly, especially in the areas that the dog frequents, and wash the dog's bedding weekly.
> - Follow up house-cleaning with carpet shampoos and sprays to rid the house of fleas at all stages of development. Insect growth regulators are the safest option.

basis. These include fipronil, imidacloprid, selamectin and permethrin (found in several formulations). Most of these products have significant flea-killing rates within 24 hours. However, none of them will control the immature forms in the environment. To accomplish this, there are a variety of insect growth regulators that can be

THE FLEA'S LIFE CYCLE

What came first, the flea or the egg? This age-old mystery is more difficult to comprehend than the actual cycle of the flea. Fleas usually live only about four months. A female can lay 2,000 eggs in her lifetime.

Egg

After ten days of rolling around your carpet or under your furniture, the eggs hatch into larvae, which feed on various and sundry debris. In days or

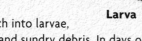

Larva

months, depending on the climate, the larvae spin cocoons and develop into the pupal or nymph stage, which quickly develop into fleas.

Pupa

These immature fleas must locate a host within 10 to 14 days or they will die. Only about 1% of the flea population exist as adult fleas, while the other 99% exist as eggs, larvae or pupae.

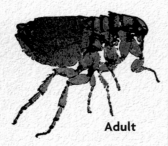

Adult

PHOTO BY CAROLINA BIOLOGICAL SUPPLY CO.

KILL FLEAS THE NATURAL WAY

If you choose not to go the route of conventional medication, there are some natural ways to ward off fleas:

- Dust your dog with a natural flea powder, composed of such herbal goodies as rosemary, wormwood, pennyroyal, citronella, rue, tobacco powder and eucalyptus.
- Apply diatomaceous earth, the fossilized remains of single-cell algae, to your carpets, furniture and pet's bedding. Even though it's not good for dogs, it's even worse for fleas, which will dry up swiftly and die.
- Brush your dog frequently, give him adequate exercise and let him fast occasionally. All of these activities strengthen the dog's system and make him more resistant to disease and parasites.
- Bathe your dog with a capful of pennyroyal or eucalyptus oil.
- Feed a natural diet, free of additives and preservatives. Add some fresh garlic and brewer's yeast to the dog's morning portion, as these items have flea-repelling properties.

sprayed into the environment (e.g., pyriproxyfen, methoprene, fenoxycarb) as well as insect development inhibitors such as lufenuron that can be administered. These compounds have no effect on adult fleas, but they stop immature forms from developing into adults. In years gone by, we relied heavily on toxic insecticides (such as organophosphates, organochlorines and carbamates) to manage the flea problem, but today's options are not only much safer to use on our pets but also safer for the environment.

TICKS

Ticks are members of the spider class (arachnids) and are blood-sucking parasites capable of transmitting a variety of diseases, including Lyme disease, ehrlichiosis, babesiosis and Rocky Mountain spotted fever. It's easy to see ticks on your own skin, but it is more of a challenge when your furry companion is affected. Whenever you happen to be planning a stroll in a tick-infested area (especially forests, grassy or wooded areas or parks) be prepared to do a thorough inspection of your dog afterward to search for ticks. Ticks can be tricky, so make sure you spend time looking in the ears, between the toes and everywhere else where a tick might hide. Ticks need to be attached for 24–72 hours before they transmit most of the diseases that they carry, so you do have a window of opportunity for some preventive intervention.

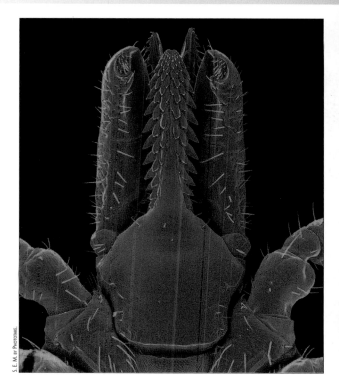

S. E. M. BY PHOTOTAKE.

A scanning electron micrograph of the head of a female deer tick, *Ixodes dammini,* a parasitic tick that carries Lyme disease.

A TICKING BOMB

There is nothing good about a tick's harpooning his nose into your dog's skin. Among the diseases caused by ticks are Rocky Mountain spotted fever, canine ehrlichiosis, canine babesiosis, canine hepatozoonosis and Lyme disease. If a dog is allergic to the saliva of a female wood tick, he can develop tick paralysis.

Female ticks live to eat and breed. They can lay between 4,000 and 5,000 eggs and they die soon after. Males, on the other hand, live only to mate with the females and continue the process as long as they are able. Most ticks live on multiple hosts before parasitizing dogs. The immature forms typically reside on grass and shrubs, waiting for susceptible animals to walk by. The larvae and nymph stages typically feed on wildlife.

If only a few ticks are present on a dog, they can be plucked out, but it is important to remove the entire head and mouthparts,

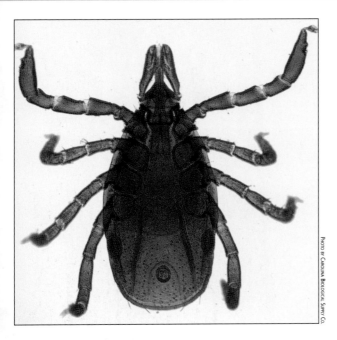

Deer tick,
Ixodes dammini.

disposed of in a container of alcohol or household bleach.

Some of the newer flea products, specifically those with fipronil, selamectin and permethrin, have effect against some, but not all, species of tick. Flea collars containing appropriate pesticides (e.g., propoxur, chlorfenvinphos) can aid in tick control. In most areas, such collars should be placed on animals in March, at the beginning of the tick season, and changed regularly. Leaving the collar on when the pesticide level is waning invites the development of resistance. Amitraz collars are also good for tick control, and the active ingredient does not interfere with other flea-control products. The ingredient helps prevent the attachment of ticks to the skin and will cause those ticks already on the skin to detach themselves.

which may be deeply embedded in the skin. This is best accomplished with forceps designed especially for this purpose; fingers can be used but should be protected with rubber gloves, plastic wrap or at least a paper towel. The tick should be grasped as closely as possible to the animal's skin and should be pulled upward with steady, even pressure. Do not squeeze, crush or puncture the body of the tick or you risk exposure to any disease carried by that tick. Once the ticks have been removed, the sites of attachment should be disinfected. Your hands should then be washed with soap and water to further minimize risk of contagion. The tick should be

TICK CONTROL

Removal of underbrush and leaf litter and the thinning of trees in areas where tick control is desired are recommended. These actions remove the cover and food sources for small animals that serve as hosts for ticks. With continued mowing of grasses in these areas, the probability of ticks' surviving is further reduced. A variety of insecticide ingredients (e.g., resmethrin, carbaryl, permethrin, chlorpyrifos, dioxathion and allethrin) are registered for tick control around the home.

MITES

Mites are tiny arachnid parasites that parasitize the skin of dogs. Skin diseases caused by mites are referred to as "mange," and there are many different forms seen in dogs. These forms are very different from one another, each one warranting an individual description.

Sarcoptic mange, or scabies, is one of the itchiest conditions that affects dogs. The microscopic *Sarcoptes* mites burrow into the superficial layers of the skin and can drive dogs crazy with itchiness. They are also communicable to people, although they can't complete their reproductive cycle on people. In addition to being tiny, the mites also are often difficult to find when trying to make a diagnosis. Skin scrapings from multiple areas are examined microscopically but, even then, sometimes the mites cannot be found.

Fortunately, scabies is relatively easy to treat, and there are a variety of products that will successfully kill the mites. Since the mites can't live in the environment for very long without feeding, a complete cure is usually possible within four to eight weeks.

Cheyletiellosis is caused by a relatively large mite, which sometimes can be seen even without a microscope. Often referred to as "walking dandruff," this also causes itching, but not usually as profound as with scabies.

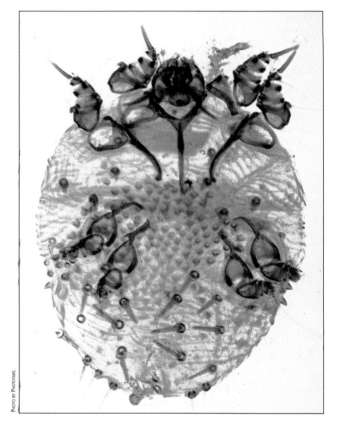

PHOTO BY PHOTOTAKE.

Sarcoptes scabiei, commonly known as the "itch mite."

While *Cheyletiella* mites can survive somewhat longer in the environment than scabies mites, they too are relatively easy to treat, being responsive to not only the medications used to treat scabies but also often to flea-control products.

Otodectes cynotis is the canine ear mite and is one of the more common causes of mange, especially in young dogs in shelters or pet stores. That's because the mites are typically present in large numbers and are quickly spread to

Micrograph of a dog louse, *Heterodoxus spiniger*. Female lice attach their eggs to the hairs of the dog. As the eggs hatch, the larval lice bite and feed on the blood. Lice can also feed on dead skin and hair. This feeding activity can cause hair loss and skin problems.

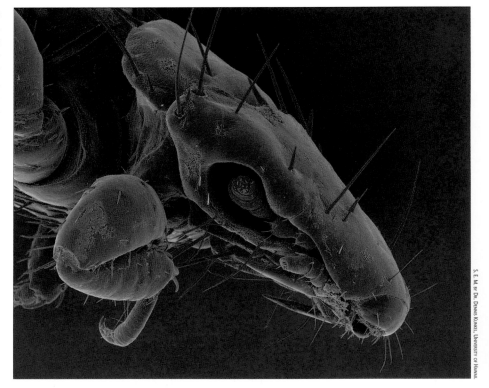

S. E. M. by Dr. Dennis Kunkel, University of Hawaii.

nearby animals. The mites rarely do much harm but can be difficult to eradicate if the treatment regimen is not comprehensive. While many try to treat the condition with ear drops only, this is the most common cause of treatment failure. Ear drops cause the mites to simply move out of the ears and as far away as possible (usually to the base of the tail) until the insecticide levels in the ears drop to an acceptable level—then it's back to business as usual! The successful treatment of ear mites requires treating all animals in the household with a systemic insecticide, such as selamectin, or a combination of miticidal ear drops combined with whole-body flea-control preparations.

Demodicosis, sometimes referred to as red mange, can be one of the most difficult forms of mange to treat. Part of the problem has to do with the fact that the mites live in the hair follicles and they are relatively well shielded from topical and systemic products. The main issue, however, is that demodectic mange typically results only when there is some underlying process interfering with the dog's immune system.

Since *Demodex* mites are

normal residents of the skin of mammals, including humans, there is usually a mite population explosion only when the immune system fails to keep the number of mites in check. In young animals, the immune deficit may be transient or may reflect an actual inherited immune problem. In older animals, demodicosis is usually seen only when there is another disease hampering the immune system, such as diabetes, cancer, thyroid problems or the use of immune-suppressing drugs. Accordingly, treatment involves not only trying to kill the mange mites but also discerning what is interfering with immune function and correcting it if possible.

Chiggers represent several different species of mite that don't parasitize dogs specifically, but do latch on to passersby and can cause irritation. The problem is most prevalent in wooded areas in the late summer and fall. Treatment is not difficult, as the mites do not complete their life cycle on dogs and are susceptible to a variety of miticidal products.

MOSQUITOES

Mosquitoes have long been known to transmit a variety of diseases to people, as well as just being biting pests during warm weather. They also pose a real risk to pets. Not only

ILLUSTRATION BY PHOTOTAKE

do they carry deadly heartworms but recently there also has been much concern over their involvement with West Nile virus. While we can avoid heartworm with the use of preventive medications, there are no such preventives for West Nile virus. The only method of prevention in endemic areas is active mosquito control. Fortunately, most dogs that have been exposed to the virus only developed flu-like symptoms and, to date, there have not been the large number of reported deaths in canines as seen in some other species.

Illustration of *Demodex folliculoram.*

MOSQUITO REPELLENT

Low concentrations of DEET (less than 10%), found in many human mosquito repellents, have been safely used in dogs but, in these concentrations, probably give only about two hours of protection. DEET may be safe in these small concentrations, but since it is not licensed for use on dogs, there is no research proving its safety for dogs. Products containing permethrin give the longest-lasting protection, perhaps two to four weeks. As DEET is not licensed for use on dogs, and both DEET and permethrin can be quite toxic to cats, appropriate care should be exercised. Other products, such as those containing oil of citronella, also have some mosquito-repellent activity, but typically have a relatively short duration of action.

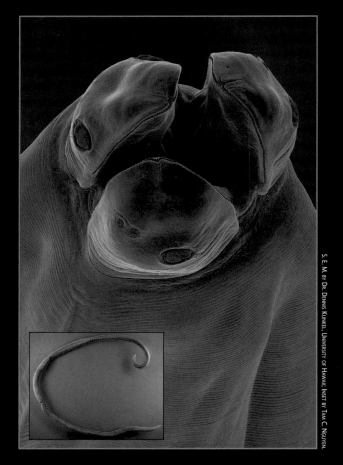

The ascarid roundworm *Toxocara canis*, showing the mouth with three lips. INSET: Photomicrograph of the roundworm *Ascaris lumbricoides*.

S. E. M. BY DR. DENNIS KUNKEL, UNIVERSITY OF HAWAII. INSET BY TAM C. NGUYEN.

INTERNAL PARASITES: WORMS

ASCARIDS

Ascarids are intestinal roundworms that rarely cause severe disease in dogs. Nonetheless, they are of major public health significance because they can be transferred to people. Sadly, it is children who are most commonly affected by the parasite, probably from inadvertently ingesting ascarid-contaminated soil. In fact, many yards and children's sandboxes contain appreciable numbers of ascarid eggs. So, while ascarids don't bite dogs or latch onto their intestines to suck blood, they do cause some nasty medical conditions in children and are best eradicated from our furry friends. Because pups can start passing ascarid eggs by three weeks of age, most parasite-control programs begin at two weeks of age and are repeated every two weeks until pups are eight weeks old. It is important to

HOOKED ON ANCYLOSTOMA

Adult dogs can become infected by the bloodsucking nematodes we commonly call hookworms via ingesting larvae from the ground or via the larvae penetrating the dog's skin. It is not uncommon for infected dogs to show no symptoms of hookworm infestation. Sometimes symptoms occur within ten days of exposure. These symptoms can include bloody diarrhea, anemia, loss of weight and general weakness. Dogs pass the hookworm eggs in their stools, which serves as the vet's method of identifying the infestation. The hookworm larvae can encyst themselves in the dog's tissues and be released when the dog is experiencing stress.

Caused by an *Ancylostoma* species whose common host is the dog, cutaneous larval migrans affects humans, causing itching and lumps and streaks beneath the surface of the skin.

S. E. M. BY DR. DENNIS KUNKEL, UNIVERSITY OF HAWAII.

realize that bitches can pass ascarids to their pups even if they test negative prior to whelping. Accordingly, bitches are best treated at the same time as the pups.

HOOKWORMS

Unlike ascarids, hookworms do latch onto a dog's intestinal tract and can cause significant loss of blood and protein. Similar to ascarids, hookworms can be transmitted to humans, where they cause a condition known as cutaneous larval migrans. Dogs can become infected either by consuming the infective larvae or by the larvae's penetrating the skin directly. People most often get infected when they are lying on the ground (such as on a beach) and the larvae penetrate the skin. Yes, the larvae can penetrate through a beach blanket. Hookworms are typically susceptible to the same medications used to treat ascarids.

The hookworm *Ancylostoma caninum* infests the intestines of dogs. INSET: Note the row of hooks at the posterior end, used to anchor the worm to the intestinal wall.

WHIPWORMS

Whipworms latch onto the lower aspects of the dog's colon and can cause cramping and diarrhea. Eggs do not start to appear in the dog's feces until about three months after the dog was infected. This worm has a peculiar life cycle, which makes it more difficult to control than ascarids or hookworms. The good thing is that whipworms rarely are transferred to people.

Some of the medications used to treat ascarids and hookworms are also effective against whipworms, but, in general, a separate treatment protocol is needed. Since most of the medications are effective against the adults but not the eggs or larvae, treatment is typically repeated in three weeks, and then often in three

Adult whipworm, *Trichuris* sp., an intestinal parasite.

S. E. M. BY DR. DENNIS KUNKEL, UNIVERSITY OF HAWAII.

WORM-CONTROL GUIDELINES
- Practice sanitary habits with your dog and home.
- Clean up after your dog and don't let him sniff or eat other dogs' droppings.
- Control insects and fleas in the dog's environment. Fleas, lice, cockroaches, beetles, mice and rats can act as hosts for various worms.
- Prevent dogs from eating uncooked meat, raw poultry and dead animals.
- Keep dogs and children from playing in sand and soil.
- Kennel dogs on cement or gravel; avoid dirt runs.
- Administer heartworm preventives regularly.
- Have your vet examine your dog's stools at your annual visits.
- Select a boarding kennel carefully so as to avoid contamination from other dogs or an unsanitary environment.
- Prevent dogs from roaming. Obey local leash laws.

months as well. Unfortunately, since dogs don't develop resistance to whipworms, it is difficult to prevent them from getting reinfected if they visit soil contaminated with whipworm eggs.

TAPEWORMS

There are many different species of tapeworm that affect dogs, but *Dipylidium caninum* is probably the most common and is spread by fleas. Flea larvae feed on organic debris and tapeworm eggs in the environment and, when a dog chews at himself and manages to ingest fleas, he might get a dose of tapeworm at the same time. The tapeworm then develops further in the intestine of the dog.

The tapeworm itself, which is a parasitic flatworm that latches onto the intestinal wall, is composed of numerous segments. When the segments break off into the intestine (as proglottids), they may accumulate around the rectum, like grains of rice. While this tapeworm is disgusting in its behavior, it is not directly communicable to humans (although humans can also get infected by swallowing fleas).

A much more dangerous flatworm is *Echinococcus multilocularis*, which is typically found in foxes, coyotes and wolves. The eggs are passed in the feces and infect rodents, and, when dogs eat the rodents, the dogs can be infected by thousands of adult tapeworms. While the parasites don't cause many problems in dogs, this is considered the most lethal worm infection that people can get. Take appropriate precautions if you live in an area in which these tapeworms are found. Do not use mulch that may contain feces of dogs, cats or wildlife, and

discourage your pets from hunting wildlife. Treat these tapeworm infections aggressively in pets, because if humans get infected, approximately half die.

HEARTWORMS

Heartworm disease is caused by the parasite *Dirofilaria immitis* and is seen in dogs around the world. A member of the roundworm group, it is spread between dogs by the bite of an infected mosquito. The mosquito injects infective larvae into the dog's skin with its bite, and these larvae develop under the skin for a period of time before making their way to the heart. There they develop into adults, which grow and create blockages of the heart, lungs and major blood vessels there. They also start producing offspring (microfilariae)

A dog tapeworm proglottid (body segment).

The dog tapeworm *Taenia pisiformis*.

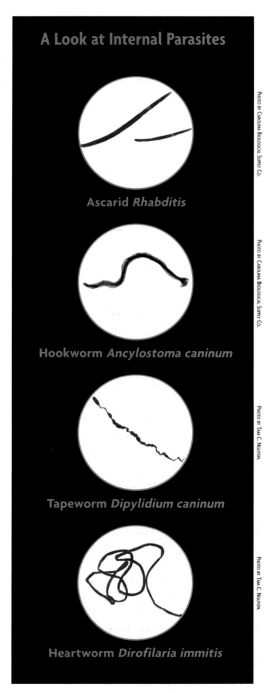

A Look at Internal Parasites

Ascarid *Rhabditis*

Hookworm *Ancylostoma caninum*

Tapeworm *Dipylidium caninum*

Heartworm *Dirofilaria immitis*

and these microfilariae circulate in the bloodstream, waiting to hitch a ride when the next mosquito bites. Once in the mosquito, the microfilariae develop into infective larvae and the entire process is repeated.

When dogs get infected with heartworm, over time they tend to develop symptoms associated with heart disease, such as coughing, exercise intolerance and potentially many other manifestations. Diagnosis is confirmed by either seeing the microfilariae themselves in blood samples or using immunologic tests (antigen testing) to identify the presence of adult heartworms. Since antigen tests measure the presence of adult heartworms and microfilarial tests measure offspring produced by adults, neither are positive until six to seven months after the initial infection. However, the beginning of damage can occur by fifth-stage larvae as early as three months after infection. Thus it is possible for dogs to be harboring problem-causing larvae for up to three months before either type of test would identify an infection.

The good news is that there are great protocols available for preventing heartworm in dogs. Testing is critical in the process, and it is important to understand the benefits as well as the limitations of such testing. All dogs six months of age or older that have not been on continuous heartworm-preventive medication should be

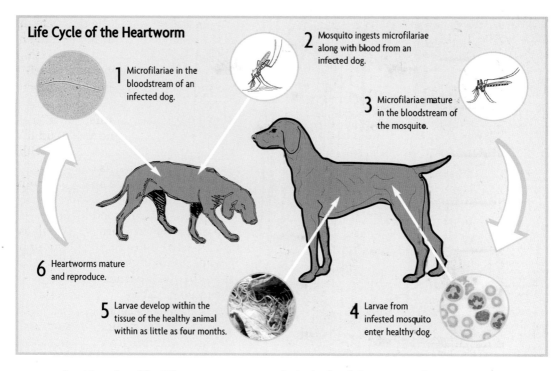

Life Cycle of the Heartworm

1 Microfilariae in the bloodstream of an infected dog.

2 Mosquito ingests microfilariae along with blood from an infected dog.

3 Microfilariae mature in the bloodstream of the mosquito.

4 Larvae from infested mosquito enter healthy dog.

5 Larvae develop within the tissue of the healthy animal within as little as four months.

6 Heartworms mature and reproduce.

screened with microfilarial or antigen tests. For dogs receiving preventive medication, periodic antigen testing helps assess the effectiveness of the preventives. The American Heartworm Society guidelines suggest that annual retesting may not be necessary when owners have absolutely provided continuous heartworm prevention. Retesting on a two- to three-year interval may be sufficient in these cases. However, your veterinarian will likely have specific guidelines under which heartworm preventives will be prescribed, and many prefer to err on the side of safety and retest annually.

It is indeed fortunate that heartworm is relatively easy to prevent, because treatments can be as life-threatening as the disease itself. Treatment requires a two-step process that kills the adult heartworms first and then the microfilariae. Prevention is obviously preferable; this involves a once-monthly oral or topical treatment. The most common oral preventives include ivermectin (not suitable for some breeds), moxidectin and milbemycin oxime; the once-a-month topical drug selamectin provides heartworm protection in addition to flea, tick and other parasite controls.

SHOWING YOUR

FOX TERRIER

Is dog showing in your blood? Are you excited by the idea of gaiting your handsome Fox Terrier around the ring to the thunderous applause of an enthusiastic audience? Are you certain that your beloved Fox Terrier is flawless? You are not alone! Every loving owner thinks that his dog has no faults, or too few to mention. No matter how many times an owner reads the breed standard, he cannot find any faults in his aristocratic companion dog. If this sounds like you, and if you are considering entering your Fox Terrier in a dog show, here are some basic questions to ask yourself:

- Did you purchase a "show-quality" puppy from the breeder?
- Is your puppy at least six months of age?
- Does the puppy exhibit correct show type for his breed?
- Does your puppy have any disqualifying faults?
- Is your Fox Terrier registered with the American Kennel Club?
- How much time do you have to devote to training, grooming, conditioning and exhibiting your dog?
- Do you understand the rules and regulations of a dog show?
- Do you have time to learn how to show your dog properly?
- Do you have the financial resources to invest in showing your dog?
- Will you show the dog yourself or hire a professional handler?
- Do you have a vehicle that can accommodate your weekend trips to the dog shows?

Success in the show ring requires more than a pretty face, a waggy tail and a pocketful of liver.

MEET THE AKC

The American Kennel Club is the main governing body of the dog sport in the United States. Founded in 1884, the AKC consists of 500 or more independent dog clubs plus 4,500 affiliated clubs, all of which follow the AKC rules and regulations. Additionally, the AKC maintains a registry for pure-bred dogs in the US and works to preserve the integrity of the sport and its continuation in the country. Over 1,000,000 dogs are registered each year, representing about 150 recognized breeds. There are over 15,000 competitive events held annually for which over 2,000,000 dogs enter to participate. Dogs compete to earn over 40 different titles, from Champion to Companion Dog to Master Agility Champion.

Even though dog shows can be exciting and enjoyable, the sport of conformation makes great demands on the exhibitors and the dogs. Winning exhibitors live for their dogs, devoting time and money to their dogs' presentation,

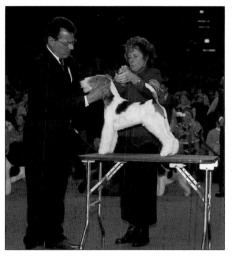

Presenting the Wire Fox Terrier in the ring requires experience and know-how. To compete with the pros, a handler has to be able to condition, groom, train and handle the dog to look his best. This Fox Terrier is being examined by the judge.

PURPLE AND GOLD HERITAGE

The Westminster Kennel Club show, America's most prestigious dog show, gained its name from the founders' favorite Manhattan hotel bar where they gathered to discuss their sporting ventures. Another theory about the name comes from a Pointer named Juno, who came from the kennel of the Duke of Westminster in England. Although Juno participated in the first show in 1877, the Duke's kennel name likely had less bearing on the choice of the club's name than did the gentlemen's celebrated watering hole. Juno, by the way, is not the Pointer in the Westminster symbol: that Pointer was a celebrated show dog by the name of Sensation, who was owned by the club.

Today the Westminster Kennel Club dog show is the oldest uninterrupted annual dog show in the world, and the second oldest sporting event in America. The first show was held on May 8-10, 1877 at Gilmore's Garden, the famous Hippodrome, with an entry of over 1200 dogs. Presently the show is held in the month of February at Madison Square Garden in New York City with an entry of 2,500 champion dogs and is televised nationally.

conditioning and training. Very few novices, even those with good dogs, will find themselves in the winners' circle, though it does happen. Don't be disheartened, though. Every exhibitor began as a novice and worked his way up to the Group ring. It's the "working your way up" part that you must keep in mind.

Assuming that you have purchased a puppy of the correct type and quality for showing, let's begin to examine the world of showing and what's required to get started. Although the entry fee into a dog show is nominal, there are lots of other hidden costs involved with "finishing" your Fox Terrier, that is, making him a champion. Things like equipment, travel, training and conditioning all cost money. A more serious campaign will include fees for a professional handler, boarding, cross-country travel and advertising. Top-winning

GROUP FIRST
TAMPA BAY
TERRIER CLUB
JULY 2004
MEYER PHOTO
By Don

it's certainly much better than a deer tick! Soon you will be envisioning yourself in the center ring at the Westminster Kennel Club Dog Show in New York City, competing for the prestigious Best in Show cup. This magical dog show is televised annually from Madison Square Garden, and the victorious dog becomes a celebrity overnight.

AKC CONFORMATION SHOWING
Visiting a dog show as a spectator is a great place to start. Pick up the show catalog to find out what time your breed is being shown, who is judging the breed and in which ring the classes will be held. To start, Fox Terriers compete against other Fox Terriers, and the winner is selected as Best of Breed by the judge. This is the procedure for each breed. At a group show, all of the Best of Breed winners go on to compete for Group One in their respective group. For example, all Best of Breed winners in a given group compete against each other; this is done for all seven groups. Finally, all seven group winners go head to head in the ring for the Best in Show award.

What most spectators don't understand is the basic idea of conformation. A dog show is often referred as a "conformation" show. This means that the judge should decide how each dog stacks up (conforms) to the breed standard for his given breed: how well does this

Ch. Kathrich Foxhollow Best of Santeric, a multiple-Group and Best in Show Wire, winning a Group 1 under judge Dr. Samuel Draper.

show dogs can represent a very considerable investment—over $100,000 has been spent in campaigning some dogs. (The investment can be less, of course, for owners who don't use professional handlers.)

Many owners, on the other hand, enter their "average" Fox Terriers in dog shows for the fun and enjoyment of it. Dog showing makes an absorbing hobby, with many rewards for dogs and owners alike. If you're having fun, meeting other people who share your interests and enjoying the overall experience, you likely will catch the "bug." Once the dog-show bug bites, its effects can last a lifetime;

FOR MORE INFORMATION....

For reliable up-to-date information about registration, dog shows and other canine competitions, contact one of the national registries by mail or via the Internet.

American Kennel Club
5580 Centerview Dr., Raleigh, NC 27606-3390
www.akc.org

United Kennel Club
100 E. Kilgore Road, Kalamazoo, MI 49002
www.ukcdogs.com

Canadian Kennel Club
89 Skyway Ave., Suite 100, Etobicoke, Ontario M9W 6R4 Canada
www.ckc.ca

The Kennel Club
1-5 Clarges St., Piccadilly, London W1Y 8AB, UK
www.the-kennel-club.org.uk

Fox Terrier conform to the ideal representative detailed in the standard? Ideally, this is what happens. In reality, however, this ideal often gets slighted as the judge compares Fox Terrier #1 to Fox Terrier #2. Again, the ideal is that each dog is judged based on his merits in comparison to his breed standard, not in comparison to the other dogs in the ring. It is easier for judges to compare dogs of the same breed to decide which they think is the better specimen; in the Group and Best in Show ring, however, it is very difficult to compare one breed to another, like apples to oranges. Thus the dog's conforma-

tion to the breed standard—not to mention advertising dollars and good handling—is essential to success in conformation shows. The dog described in the standard (the standard for each AKC breed is written and approved by the breed's national parent club and then submitted to the AKC for approval) is the perfect dog of that breed, and breeders keep their eye on the standard when they choose which dogs to breed, hoping to get closer and closer to the ideal with each litter.

Another good first step for the novice is to join a dog club. You will be astonished by the many and different kinds of dog clubs in the country, with about 5,000 clubs holding events every year. Most clubs require that prospective new members present two letters of recommendation from existing members. Perhaps you've made

The Smooths and the Wires compete in separate classes as separate breeds in AKC shows. Here's a class of lovely Smooths competing for the ribbon.

EXPRESS YOURSELF
The most intangible of all canine attributes, expression speaks to the character of the breed, attained by the combined features of the head. The shape and balance of the dog's skull, the color and position of the eyes and the size and carriage of the head mingle to produce the correct expression of the breed. A judge may approach a dog and determine instantly whether the dog's face portrays the desired impression for the breed, conveying nobility, intelligence and alertness among other specifics of the breed standard.

some friends visiting a show held by a particular club and you would like to join that club. Dog clubs may specialize in a single breed, like a local or regional Fox Terrier club, or in a specific pursuit, such as obedience, tracking or hunting tests. There are all-breed clubs for all-dog enthusiasts; they sponsor special training days, seminars on topics like grooming or handling or lectures on breeding or canine genetics. There are also clubs that specialize in certain types of dogs, like herding dogs, hunting dogs, companion dogs, etc.

A parent club is the national organization, sanctioned by the AKC, which promotes and safeguards its breed in the country. The American Fox Terrier Club was formed in 1885 and can be contacted on the Internet at www.aftc.org. The parent club holds an annual national specialty show, usually in a different city each year, in which many of the country's top dogs, handlers and breeders gather to compete. At a specialty show, only members of a single breed are invited to participate. There are also Group specialties, in which all members of a Group are invited. For more information about dog clubs in your area, contact the AKC at www.akc.org on the Internet or write them at their Raleigh, NC address.

OTHER TYPES OF COMPETITION
In addition to conformation shows, the AKC holds a variety of other competitive events. Obedience trials, agility trials and tracking trials are open to all breeds, while hunting tests, field trials, lure coursing, herding tests and trials, earthdog tests and coonhound events are limited to specific breeds or groups of breeds. The Junior Showmanship program is offered to

aspiring young handlers and their dogs, and the Canine Good Citizen® program is an all-around good-behavior test open to all dogs, pure-bred and mixed.

OBEDIENCE TRIALS

Mrs. Helen Whitehouse Walker, a Standard Poodle fancier, can be credited with introducing obedience trials to the United States. In the 1930s she designed a series of exercises based on those of the Associated Sheep, Police, Army Dog Society of Great Britain. These exercises were intended to evaluate the working relationship between dog and owner. Since those early days of the sport in the US, obedience trials have grown more and more popular, and now more than 2,000 trials each year attract over 100,000 dogs and their owners. Any dog registered with the AKC, regardless of neutering or other disqualifications that would preclude entry in conformation competition, can participate in obedience trials.

There are three levels of difficulty in obedience competition. The first (and easiest) level is the Novice, in which dogs can earn the Companion Dog (CD) title. The intermediate level is the Open level, in which the Companion Dog Excellent (CDX) title is awarded. The advanced level is the Utility level, in which dogs compete for the Utility Dog (UD) title. Classes at each level are further divided into

"A" and "B," with "A" for beginners and "B" for those with more experience. In order to win a title at a given level, a dog must earn three "legs." A "leg" is accomplished when a dog scores 170 or higher (200 is a perfect score). The scoring system gets a little trickier when you understand that a dog must score more than 50% of the points available for each exercise in order to actually earn the points. Available points for each exercise range between 20 and 40.

A dog must complete different exercises at each level of obedience. The Novice exercises are the easiest, with the Open and finally the Utility levels progressing in difficulty. Examples of Novice exercises are on- and off-lead heeling, a figure-8 pattern, performing a recall (or come), long sit and long down and standing for examination. In the Open level, the Novice-level exercises are required again, but this time without a leash and for longer durations. In addition, the dog must clear a broad jump, retrieve over a jump and drop on recall. In the Utility level, the exercises are quite difficult, including executing basic commands based on hand signals, following a complex heeling pattern, locating articles based on scent discrimination and completing jumps at the handler's direction.

Once he's earned the UD title, a dog can go on to win the prestigious title of Utility Dog Excellent (UDX) by winning "legs" in ten shows. Additionally, Utility Dogs who win "legs" in Open B and Utility B earn points toward the lofty title of Obedience Trial Champion (OTCh.). Established in 1977 by the AKC, this title requires a dog to earn 100 points as well as three first places in a combination of Open B and Utility B classes under three different judges. The "brass ring" of obedience competition is the AKC's National Obedience Invitational. This is an exclusive competition for only the cream of the obedience crop. In order to qualify for the invitational, a dog must be ranked in either the top 25 all-breeds in obedience or in the top three for his breed in obedience. The title at stake here is that of National Obedience Champion (NOC).

AGILITY TRIALS

Agility trials became sanctioned by the AKC in August 1994, when the first licensed agility trials were held. Since that time, agility certainly has grown in popularity by leaps and bounds, literally! The AKC allows all registered breeds (including Miscellaneous Class breeds) to participate, providing the dog is 12 months of age or older. Agility is designed so that the handler demonstrates how well the dog can work at his side. The handler directs his dog through, over, under and around an obstacle course that includes jumps, tires, the dog walk, weave poles, pipe tunnels, collapsed tunnels and more. While working his way through the course, the dog must keep one eye and ear on the handler and the rest of his body on the course. The handler runs along with the dog, giving verbal and hand signals to guide the dog through the course.

The first organization to promote agility trials in the US was the United States Dog Agility Association, Inc. (USDAA). Established in 1986, the USDAA sparked the formation of many member clubs around the country. To participate in USDAA trials, dogs must be at least 18 months of age.

The USDAA and AKC both offer titles to winning dogs, although the exercises and requirements of the two organizations differ. Agility Dog (AD), Advanced Agility Dog (AAD) and Master Agility Dog (MAD) are the titles offered by the USDAA, while the AKC offers Novice Agility (NA), Open Agility (OA), Agility Excellent (AX) and Master Agility Excellent (MX). Beyond these four AKC titles, dogs can win additional titles in "jumper" classes: Jumper with Weave Novice (NAJ), Open (OAJ) and Excellent (MXJ). The ultimate title in AKC agility is MACH, Master Agility Champion. Dogs can continue to add number designations to the MACH title, indicating how many times the dog has met the title's requirements (MACH1, MACH2 and so on).

Agility trials are a great way to keep your dog active, and they will keep you running, too! You should join a local agility club to learn more about the sport. These clubs offer sessions in which you can introduce your dog to the various obstacles as well as training classes to prepare him for competition. In no time, your dog will be climbing A-frames, crossing the dog walk and flying over hurdles, all with you right beside him. Your heart will leap every time your dog jumps through the hoop—and you'll be having just as much (if not more) fun!

EARTHDOG EVENTS

Earthdog trials are held for those breeds that were developed to "go to ground." These dogs were bred to go down into badger and fox holes and bring out the quarry. Breeds such as Parson Russell Terriers, Dachshunds and other short-legged hunters are used in this fashion. Earthdog trials test the dog in a simulated hunting situation in which trenches are dug and lined, usually with wood. The scent of a rat is laid in the trench, and the quarry is a caged rat at the end of the tunnel. The dog can see and smell the rat but cannot touch or harm the quarry in any way.

There are four levels in earthdog trials. The first, Introduc-

tion to Quarry, is for beginners and uses a 10-foot tunnel. No title is awarded at this level. The Junior Earthdog (JE) title is awarded at the next level, which uses a 30-foot tunnel with three 90-degree turns. Two qualifying JE runs are required for a dog to earn the title. The next level, Senior Earthdog (SE), uses the same length tunnel and number of turns as in the JE level, but also has a false den and exit and requires the dog to come out of the tunnel when called. To try for the SE title, a dog must have at least his JE; the SE title requires three qualifying runs at this level. The most difficult of the earthdog tests, Master Earthdog (ME), again uses the 30-foot tunnel with three 90-degree turns, with a false entrance, exit and den. The dog is required to enter in the right place and, in this test, honor another working dog. The ME title requires four qualifying runs, and a dog must have earned his SE title to attempt the ME level.

At an agility event, one of the hardest obstacles for the "get-up-and-go" Fox Terrier is known as the pause table, which is 12 inches off the ground. The dog must stay there for five seconds: when the dog assumes the correct position, the judge counts "4, 3, 2, 1, Go!"

INDEX

𝕸𝔂 𝔉𝔬𝔵 𝕿𝔢𝔯𝔯𝔦𝔢𝔯

PUT YOUR PUPPY'S FIRST PICTURE HERE

Dog's Name _____

Date _____ Photographer _____